WITCH

*Divine Alignments with the Primordial
Energies of Magick and Cycles of Nature*

Enjoy these other books in the Common Sentience series:

AKASHA: *Spiritual Experiences of Accessing the Infinite Intelligence of Our Souls*

ANCESTORS: *Divine Remembrances of Lineage, Relations and Sacred Sites*

ANGELS: *Personal Encounters with Divine Beings of Light*

ANIMALS: *Personal Tales of Encounters with Spirit Animals*

ASCENSION: *Divine Stories of Awakening the Whole and Holy Being Within*

GODTALK: *Experiences of Humanity's Connections with a Higher Power*

GUIDES: *Mystical Connections to Soul Guides and Divine Teachers*

MEDITATION: *Intimate Experiences with the Divine through Contemplative Practices*

NATURE: *Divine Experiences with Trees, Plants, Stones and Landscapes*

SHAMANISM: *Personal Quests of Communion with Nature and Creation*

SIGNS: *Sacred Encounters with Pathways, Turning Points, and Divine Guideposts*

SOUND: *Profound Experiences with Chanting, Toning, Music and Healing Frequencies*

Learn more at sacredstories.com.

WITCH

Divine Alignments with the Primordial Energies of Magick and Cycles of Nature

VALERIE LOVE

SACRED STORIES
PUBLISHING

Witch:
Divine Alignments with the Primordial Energies of Magick and Cycles of Nature

Valerie Love

Print ISBN: 978-1-958921-31-9
EBook ISBN: 978-1-958921-32-6

Library of Congress Control Number: 2023940660

Published by Sacred Stories Publishing, Fort Lauderdale, FL USA

CONTENTS

PART THREE: DEEPENING YOUR RELATIONSHIP WITH THE WITCH

MEET THE SACRED STORYTELLERS

MEET THE AUTHOR

PART ONE

Understanding the Witch

The witch is a person who has made a conscious choice to embrace their own power.

— DOREEN VALIENTE

I AM WITCH

———•———•———•———

I am the darkness which defies comprehension.
I am the light which heals all.

I am at home with both death and birth, blood and bones,
tears and agony, joy and ecstasy.

I am the waxing and waning of the moon, the ebb and flow of
ocean tides and streaming waters.

I am the cycle of life, the seasons of awakening and sleep,
and the currents and tides of all existence.

I am primordial, ancient, mysterious, formidable,
and exquisite.

I am the wielder of immense power and the destroyer
of old worlds.

I AM WITCH.

I do not seek to please or coerce. I am a force all my own.

I am known to those who seek me in the wood, the leaf, the moon,
the wind, the waters, the dancing firelight and in all my abodes.

I knock, yet must be invited in.

Those who are my own have welcomed me
and persist in honoring me inside their own being,
in their holy crypts, and everywhere they traverse.

I seek initiates, yet receive only the willing.
My doors are open to all, though few dare enter.

I summon my initiates with a gentle, unabating whisper in
the fiery cauldron of the immortal heart: Rise witch, rise.

I tutor the lost ones, those ignorant of the ways of the craft,
and the uninitiated—only if they are willing to endure
the searing transmutation I require for them to be awarded
the abilities to peer into mysteries beyond the domain of humans,
change the outcomes and destinies of men, and
operate unfettered outside the bounds of time.

I AM WITCH.

I heal. I cure. I birth. I destroy. I am the hands, feet, voice,
and will of the Goddess inhabiting inclined souls.

I am the force transmuting the decaying corpse into a
dandelion even as it is enveloped by the Earth Mother.

I am the urge of the newborn babe to suckle at its mother's breast.

I hold all elements within my purview—earth, air, fire,
water—and activate the same for my devotees to use at their
will to effect powerful magick.

I dwell in the huts of my adherents with drying herbs
hanging from the rafters, or stewing in glass jars to become
oils, tinctures, and potions.

I frequent the lair of the midwife and the cut wife,
guiding their deft hands.

I AM WITCH.

I am an ancient archetype, alive and thriving in the deep unconscious
of all who live or have ever lived and those yet
to be born.

I am the phoenix, a crucible of proof that what was once
burned was never lost.

I influence all. Nothing in existence is hidden from me.

I am the abiding presence and aspect of the Goddess
who walks among the living.

I am the deep urge to know, heal, teach, birth, destroy,
and begin anew.

I do not hesitate, nor am I afraid of anything.

I am the power accessible only to those who are my expressions
on the earth plane.

I am the bornless, deathless, breathless power of eternal being.

I AM WITCH.

A PRIMORDIAL POWER EMERGES

———•———•———•———

In the dark crypt of being, a primordial power older than time and vaster than the stars undulates and swirls, urging all life ever onward in its harmonious, perfect cycles and seasons, underpinning all existence. A bequest and creation of the Goddess, this power operates at her behest, serving as emissary, teacher, healer, and wayshower to humankind.

This potent power is an enduring, ancient archetype, accessible in the boundless unconscious by those who dare to delve into occult regions existing beyond space, time, and the confines of the third dimension.

Others have met this power in her aspect as keeper of nature in the shadow of the wood, where trees whisper their sweet secrets; in the falling autumn leaf, the glistening silver of the moon, the whip of the wind, the streams of waters, both salty and sweet, and the dancing firelight casting shadows upon the faces that behold it.

This potent power and primordial force—the ancient archetype, emissary of the Goddess, keeper of nature, wisdom teacher, healer, and wayshower—is the witch.

The witch is a wielder of power. Raw. Unmitigated. Undifferentiated.

Though she is hidden, the witch whispers a secret call to her would-be initiates from the cauldron of the heart. Accessible by all, yet answered by few, the call bids us to enter a shadowy world to explore and understand the multi-faceted, enigmatic, wildly popular powerhouse that is witch.

The witch has been with us for thousands of years, and she'll be with us for thousands more. She is both magickal and mystical, sparking the imagination and lore of humans for eons. Some consider her a helper to humanity while others see her as a foe. How admirers or detractors choose to consider the witch has no effect on the enduring pinnacle of magick she is or the power she wields, or the influence she has on consciousness and the activities of humans in every sphere of endeavor.

The witch touches us all.

When one answers the call of the witch from deep within, worlds open and new energies reveal themselves, though they were present all along as undetected potentialities. One finds their connection with the witch to be an empowering adjunct to all human actions, causing outcomes beyond what can be expected by simply performing tasks. If one fully succumbs to the witch within, each human action becomes infused with magick, wonder, and potency, often creating non-ordinary and supernatural results. The witch exploits synchronicity for its dynamic organizing and timing power. What we once thought impossible becomes doable and natural; that which we once viewed as occult, hidden, secret, and the unknowable reveals itself in full array over time, with stunning accuracy, as one dares to venture deeper.

Witch is a way of being, existing in the core of the spirit, heart, mind, bones, and blood of those who have chosen to welcome her in, and who own and embody this incomprehensible power.

When courage prompts us to say *yes* to the inner witch, a knowing arises. One who knows herself as a witch is aware of the unmitigated power residing within, along with the right and responsibility to use it. A witch knows that all is connected through a great web of life. Anything that affects one aspect of the web affects the whole. This power is to be wielded only after training and achieving proficiency.

Because the witch is an emissary of the Goddess, she stirs, awakens, and activates latent gifts, energies, and potentialities in those who come under her tutelage. The gifts are used according to intention and will. She can peer into the future, parallel universes, and worlds unknown to those who are not able to access this important information. The witch also can serve humanity in a plethora of ways, to include employing magick and witchcraft to create, transform, and eliminate.

GIFTS OF THE WITCH

What are the gifts of the witch? They include the "clears:"

- Clairvoyance (clear seeing)
- Clairaudience (clear hearing)
- Claircognizance (clear knowing)
- Clairsentience (clear feeling)

Other gifts that the Divine has bestowed upon witches include the precognition of information, which appears as images in the third eye or in the dream state. Witches can access the ability to *divine*, to know the mind of God with the aid of tools such as Tarot cards; rune symbols carved with intention on stones, which were originally used by Germanic peoples; tea leaves; bones; cowrie shells, used by West African peoples to access the wisdom of the ancestors, spirits, and gods or Orisha; dowsing rods; crystal balls; the planets and stars; and pendulums.

Mediumship—the ability to commune with spirits who have left the third dimension and abide in dimensions beyond—is a domain of the witch. A famed example of a witch skilled in mediumship is the Witch of Endor from the Holy Bible, who was able to conjure the spirit of Samuel and view him clearly, complete with the clothing he'd worn in his human life. She ascertained all information from the dead prophet accurately, including predictions that were fulfilled in short order.

Witches commune and experience companionship with nature and nature spirits. We use this powerful gift to understand the workings of the universe, inform our spellwork, and make our rituals both potent and memorable. A deep, visceral understanding and desire to connect and commune with nature in all its forms—the essence of trees, plants, herbs, flowers, roots, fruits, vegetables, wind, storms, streams, rivers, oceans, stones, mountains, caves, animals, birds, and insects—factors into the life, walk, and workings of the witch and her craft. The witch understands a simple truth: What you love will tell you its secrets. A witch loves nature, and therefore, the secrets of nature are revealed to her.

In my walk as a witch, I hold two truths dear:

First, *all is Divine.* Reverence for all life, in its manifold and splendid forms, is a code for me and for many other witches. Countless witches adhere, as best we can, to the edict to "harm none." As is taught in the mystery school I founded, "harm none" goes far beyond not swatting at a fly or stomping on an insect. We seek to subscribe to the principle of *ahimsa*, a Sanskrit word that means to not inflict injury but also has a deeper occult meaning.

"Ahimsa means not to injure any creature by thought, word, or deed," taught Gandhi. The principle of harmlessness is the same for witches. Those who adhere to the principle of harmlessness have chosen to treat all life as sacred and as an expression of the Divine. Our reverence for life elicits awe. To walk upon the earth as a beneficial presence—and not simply as someone who does no harm—is to practice *ahimsa.* Some witches undertake a vow of harmlessness; I took my vow many years ago in a sacred initiation, in which I swore an oath to the All that I would not only refrain from intentionally causing harm, but I would intend and actively become a universal force for good.

The second truth I hold dear as a witch is that my mind, will, words, and actions form the ultimate magick wand. I can employ these things to effect change in the physical universe and in any sphere of life experience.

Though she utilizes a plethora of accoutrement, a witch knows *she* is the power, even without a wand, crystals, incense, or any other tool. The power resides in and of the witch and can be accessed and channeled to heal, transform, correct, and/or eliminate crossed conditions. The witch can direct, with intention and will, the potent and palpable energies at her disposal. We will discuss many of those energies here.

Welcome to the world of the witch and the mysteries inherent in this ancient archetype. We shall explore both with an intention to shed light in the darkness, so we emerge with wisdom regarding this primordial force.

HONORING THE ANCESTORS

━━━━●━━━━●━━━━●━━━━

I am Valerie, daughter of Jacqueline, daughter of Frieda, daughter of Pinky, daughter of Dell. Great honor, homage, and gratitude goes forth from my heart and rises to the souls and wombs that caused and effectuated my birth, life, and path. In my lineage, it is paramount for us to always honor our ancestors. It is said that our ancestors form a ladder to the Divine.

I am from a long line of witches who employed and mastered natural healing methodologies to treat the body temple as well as the emotions, mind, and spirit. These skilled healers did not turn to doctors or outside professionals, but to intuition, gut, hunches, moon cycles, dreams, premonitions, cloud patterns, and moisture in the air. They concocted pot liquor, liniments, poultices, rubs, ointments, oils, and tinctures; they used herbs, plants, roots, salts, berries, and more items from nature than could be recounted and described in one book.

They had dreams about fish and knew who was pregnant long before anyone took a pregnancy test. They midwifed babies and taped copper pennies on the bellies of the ones who had protruding belly buttons that wouldn't go down. Their results were better than those of formally trained medical professionals.

Being kitchen witches and hedge witches, they grew herbs in the garden and plants in the home, which they spoke to and treated like members of the family. Their first go-to for any ailment that arose was plants and potions, not doctors.

They were strange and untamed, as the witch often is, with unruly hair that they always flushed down the toilet when they brushed or combed it; they issued the admonition to us children to "never let anyone get ahold of your hair." They knew that ill-intentioned root-workers and folk magick practitioners wrought powerful cunning with anything they could acquire from the body of their target, including clipped nails and shed hair.

They prayed and made things come true, like getting people out of jail or getting them jobs. They lived with spirits in their houses and weren't concerned, because the spirits seemed to abide by the rules of the roost. They talked to "dead" people.

Amid all their bizarre rituals—throwing dishwater in the direction of the sun, drawing salt circles and lines, keeping High John the Conqueror root in a pocket for protection, communing with spirits, employing telepathy, and giving heed to precognition received in dreams—my ancestors never called themselves "witches," nor did they refer to their practices as "witchcraft." *Magick* was a natural way of being for my forebears. They never considered being any way other than magickal, and they passed this attitude down through the generations.

I didn't know any other way of being other than what I had witnessed and experienced. As a young girl growing up in Harlem, New York, I thought everyone operated this way. It wasn't until much later in my spiritual walk—after I'd read a mountain of books on the craft, magick, and the occult—that I recognized what these practices our family engaged in truly were. I realized there was a name for what we were doing.

It's called witchcraft.

We were witches? Yes. We were witches.

To call the discovery shocking would be to minimize the feeling that slowly engulfed me as it gradually sank in. *We're witches. I am a witch.*

The more I studied witchcraft and the rules of magick, the more I accepted the realization that we had been practicing witchcraft and magick all along. Maybe your forebears were witches, too. You might be able to spot witchcraft in your family's heritage, traditions, and "old wives' tales." Witchcraft is ubiquitous. Not many families have escaped it altogether.

Why are magickal practices and witchcraft so prevalent? Because they work. As practical and real as life, magick and witchcraft have provided solutions to issues concerning all humanity: love, money, career, and health. For all practical life matters, witchcraft has answers, which explains its enduring and undeniable appeal.

The surge in interest and in the practice of magick and witchcraft has bloomed over the last few decades. Store shelves now burst with books on the witch that would not have been found even twenty years ago. Crystal shops abound, and more people than ever understand their power. The witchy aesthetic has gained ground in mainstream media; it is no longer considered life-threatening to publicly declare oneself a witch.

Even in this modern, scientific age, we are enamored with the witch and her ability to solve real-world problems. My ancestors helped me understand some vital truths about the witch and her workings:

Witchcraft can be simple. It can be as simple as saying a prayer or incantation over a homemade remedy and rubbing someone down with it. The witches I hail from used simple, practical magick. It had to work for it to be employed repeatedly.

Witchcraft is an orientation. It is a way of looking at the world and all in it, more than it is one specific thing one has to do. Knowing what to do issues from deep within one's being. Imagination is a partner of the witch. The witches I'm from understood the fundamental principles of the energies and correspondences they were working with. They used their ingenuity, wit, wisdom, and knowledge of the natural world to create health-sustaining, harmonizing practices for self, the body, the home, and for whatever ailed someone.

Witchcraft is unique to every witch. Yes, there was a flavor and flair to all the witches in my family—yet each was powerfully her own being. I come from powerhouse women, and men as well, who rarely fit in or saw a need to. By its very definition, being a witch means one does *not* fit in. A witch is a self-initiating agent of change.

Witchcraft is in the blood. As a woman of African descent on my mother's side, and Puerto Rican descent on my father's side, all the African magicks live in my blood, including Yoruba and Santeria, though I've never been initiated into either. When I'm in those circles, I understand their energy on a soul level.

Magick is in our blood. Magick may be in your blood, too, even if you're not aware of a lineage of witches. If you aspire to a higher magickal practice and more potent witchcraft, you may look no further than your ancestry to provide you with all the magick you'll ever require. I'm not solely referring to the obvious aspects of ancestry. My DNA contains a healthy dose of Scottish, which explains why I've always been drawn to Scottish witchcraft, even though I look like a black woman in this incarnation.

In our traditions and rites, we honor our ancestors, speak their names, and hold them in high regard. In some witchcraft circles and rituals, we introduce ourselves by stating our name and our matriarchal lineage as far back as we know it; that's why I wrote the introduction to this chapter in that way.

To honor the witch is to recognize her hallmarks wherever they appear. We may need to look no further than our own lineage and the practices our families hold dear to find the footsteps of the witch.

WITCHCRAFT AND MAGICK

———•———•———•———

O f the countless expressions of the witch and the witch's cultivated power, most have heard of witchcraft and magick. Existence expresses. An expression of the existence of the witch is witchcraft and magick.

WITCHCRAFT

As a witch, I use witchcraft in three broad categories that contain the potential for experiences we deeply desire as humans. Many of us want the same things: an aligned and perfect partner; to be a parent; to have greater resources and enjoy all they can afford us; to be vibrant and happy; and to be peaceful and fulfilled in all ways. We long for states of being that are desirable, and we avidly seek solutions to the painful problems in life we all encounter. For these purposes, I use witchcraft.

CREATION

Witchcraft is an age-old means to manifest new creations into reality by using magick to aid her words, actions, and endeavors. The witch knows that spiritual work is required—along with the requisite mental, emotional, and physical involvement—to bring anything new into manifestation.

A witch uses creation magick to birth new things, conditions, and experiences into reality. Examples include:

> **Babies**: In cultures around the world, a person who has a desire to have children and has encountered challenges with doing so might consult a witch. While witches do not have the cure for infertility, and babies can only enter the world after a long chain of complex physical actions and reactions, there are important spiritual or energetic components to becoming pregnant. The spiritual essence that makes birth possible is the pool of the witch.

> **Business**: An empowered, experienced witch who knows cosmic timing well can help clients with the optimal start of a new business venture. The witch also can offer altar work, candle magick, appropriate herbs, prayers, spells, talismans, and amulets among other magickal aids to help successfully birth the new venture.

> **Love**: Properly executed witchcraft can help secure a new relationship with a perfectly aligned mate. Of course, one would still have to take steps on the physical plane to meet a potential mate. Yet a witch can help to unravel the spiritual and energetic reasons why such a relationship may not have unfolded yet.

TRANSMUTATION

Witchcraft also can be used handily to change, transform, or transmute. There are experiences we may be having that are fulfilling to some extent yet are not optimal. We may desire a change in circumstances or experience to make these situations more desirable or more fulfilling, such as:

Deeper connection: An experienced witch can help with sweetening a relationship. You may have the right partner, and things are going well, yet you both realize the relationship could be a lot better. You both desire a transformation into more desirable states of interacting with each other. Perhaps you desire greater peace in the relationship, or deeper and more understanding communication, or better sex and intimacy. A witch can help with all aspects of sweetening a relationship.

Better business: A witch in the field of business can help business enterprises scale rapidly, to gain far more clients and customers and the resultant profits. Witchcraft for business expansion does not obviate the need for changes in the business to produce greater profitability, but it does offer spiritual and energetic advantages. With the help of spirit entities, moon cycles, herbs, altar work, candles, and more, a witch can favorably move the existing business upward rapidly and demonstrably, without downside traps that could take place with rapid business acceleration.

Space cleansing: A common reason witches are sought out is to change the energy or atmosphere of a home, especially in homes where untoward events have occurred. A commanding witch transmutes energy by means of suffumigation with incense and sage and will use spiritual perfumes for the energy each corresponds to. The witch also burns candles to transmute spaces from chaotic to peaceful and summons helpful spirits to anchor a sense of wellbeing in the space, by communicating with land spirits who are happy to be guardians so that peace and well-being are protected. Witches are also known to employ the use of amulets, charms, and talismans to be worn by the inhabitants of a home to assist the working.

DESTRUCTION

A third reason witches perform the craft is to destroy. Without the ability to destroy and the energies of destruction, everything ever created would still be in existence, resulting in an uninhabitable world. Just as creation is necessary for the complete cycle of life, so too are death and destruction.

Witches have the right, ability, skills, and tools to get rid of the undesirable and to make that riddance permanent. A powerful witch can counter and balance the birthing energies of new creation with the destructive energies of death. A witch can use destruction magick for:

Healing people: Getting rid of disease, sickness, and infirmity. Witches often are called on for healing, which may involve ridding the patient of negative energies in the spirit, mind, body, emotions, and home. These negative energies are not transmuted but *banished*, thus providing relief. Witches perform this healing work with herbs, incantations, candle magick, spells, and rituals.

Healing legal issues: Getting rid of negative situations, such as court cases and lawsuits. Because these can be so problematic for everyone involved, witchcraft and magick on this topic has been practiced for centuries and across cultures by people seeking beneficial outcomes and satisfying solutions to some of humanity's most pressing problems. In the witch's arsenal for banishing lawsuits and the like are spells and incantations, as well as burning candles that have been made into appropriate shapes, carved with appropriate words, and dressed with corresponding oils pertinent to the working.

Banishing unwanted spirits: Dealing with unwanted entities is another dicey situation that calls for the deft hand of a skillful practitioner. Witches who are effective in this kind of witchcraft understand the spirit world deeply and viscerally from building and maintaining relationships with spirit allies who become helpers in banishing unwanted spirits. A power tool of the witch is banishing a spirit by means of a more powerful spirit.

There are as many expressions of witchcraft and actions of the witch as there are witches. Witchcraft and the domain of the activity of the witch are in no way limited or impeded by laws of man, nor by constraints of religion and dogma, for witches work in a solitary fashion.

MAGICK

The witch who practices magick is delving into the art and science of transformation and transmutation of oneself, one's surroundings, the entire world, and the cosmos. Magick is defined as the science and art of bringing about change in conformity with the will. The "will" as used here refers to Divine urge or destiny. The will of an acorn is to become an oak tree. The will of a human is to potentialize and activate all their latent powers to become a fully realized being. Divine will is housed in the energetic system at the solar plexus chakra, also known as the "central sun," the seat of motivation that fires us into action.

This will or urge to do more and be more is present in us all, yet for many, it lies in wait as a vast, inactivated fount of power and creativity. Magick unleashes this surge of creativity and channels it from a dormant and inactivated state into tangible goods, empires, and experiences on the third-dimensional plane.

In the process, magick changes the magician. Unlike witchcraft, which has different aims, magick aims first and foremost to change the consciousness of the one performing it. From summoning spirits to evoking ancestors, every magickal act is a consciousness-expanding foray into the wild knowns and unknowns of our vast cosmos and its inhabitants, seen and unseen.

Witches who practice witchcraft may also practice magick, or vice versa, or they might practice neither. Of all the ways witches connect with and express the energy of this ancient archetype, one thing is certain: the witch can call upon all elemental, ancestral, supernatural, planetary, stellar, lunar, and cosmic powers at her disposal to influence desired outcomes.

The witch is the cause, not the effect.

Each witch has a personal brand of magick. Practicing magick is better than reading 1,000 books on practicing magick, though it's also far more challenging. While there are countless forms of magick and magickal systems—Hoodoo, Vodun, Quimbanda, Santeria, and Solomonic, to name a few—each witch is the arbiter of what is right for her.

Witches can practice any magickal system or tradition desired, based on intuitive guidance, the personal belief system, cultural background, spiritual practices, and goals. Magick and witchcraft systems that abound today include:

TRADITIONAL WITCHCRAFT

Traditional witchcraft is a term used to describe forms of witchcraft that are based on pre-Christian folk magick and beliefs. Traditional witches engage in divination, spellcasting, and herbalism, among other techniques. The witch has existed since time immemorial, and because humans have always sought supernatural answers to life's problems, witches have flourished in every age. Thus, before there were any of the practices and rituals that have come down to us today as a rich heritage, the witch pulled herbs to heal and enchant, birthed babies, danced under the moon, performed rites and ceremonies for self and others, and spent long days swooning away in the woods. Traditional witchcraft, the core of what we practice, is still alive and well, even though it may be dressed up with robes and ritual. The witch is traditional at heart and forever remembers and honors the long, unbroken line of magickal practitioners who have gone before and the magick they've bequeathed to us. We are worthy caretakers indeed.

WICCA

Though the roots of Wicca harken back to an ancient era, Gerald Gardner reached backward and forward to link the ancient ways of the witch to the modern day. He pointed the way forward with a path that witches could ascribe to and make their own. Considered by many to be the "father of Wicca," Gardner was a legendary witch who gave form, ritual, ceremony, practice, and a coven to modern Wiccans, indelibly marking the landscape of witchcraft. Gardnerian Wicca emphasizes the celebration of nature and its seasons and cycles and focuses on the masculine and feminine aspects of the Divine as the God and Goddess.

Alexandrian Wicca was founded by Alex Sanders, who was initiated into Gardnerian witchcraft but eventually broke away to form his own tradition. Alex Sanders' initiation as a child by his witch grandmother is quite a tale. Some consider Alexandrian Witchcraft as arising out of Gardnerian Witchcraft, and though the two share many of the same practices and beliefs, there are clear distinctions in ceremonies, rites, initiation, and the practice of magick.

Hierarchical in structure, Wiccan covens provide space for the burgeoning witch to find her way and move through the trials of initiation. Within the coven, the witch can learn the craft, be taught by experienced elders, and learn to practice witchcraft and magick safely. Not all Wiccans are associated with a coven. I know of fulfilled and happy solitary Wiccans who practice within the private sphere of their own sacred space.

Decades ago, when I was finding my way as a witch, I was without a clue as to where to go or what to do. I found courage, inspiring words, rituals, and practices in many books on Wicca. Each book I devoured fired my inner cauldron. Though Wicca is not a practice I personally subscribe to as a witch, it has done much to raise awareness of witches in the modern era and has inspired generations of witches to exit broom closets proudly.

HOODOO

Hoodoo is a form of African American folk magick that combines elements of African, Native American, and European magickal practices. Hoodoo practitioners use tools and techniques—such as candle magick, herbalism, and divination—to achieve their goals. They also use the book of Psalms in the Bible and books titled *The Sixth and Seventh Books of Moses*, though it's doubtful Moses actually penned the words. *The Sixth Book of Moses* contains spells, prayers, and magickal instructions, focusing on the use of Divine names and invocations to achieve desired outcomes. The book also includes information on the use of herbs, stones, and other natural materials in magickal practices. *The Seventh Book of Moses* contains more advanced magickal instructions, including how to summon spirits and angels and how to use seals and talismans in magickal workings. The book also contains prayers and psalms. Both the *Sixth and Seventh Books of Moses* have been influential in the development of folk magick and African American Hoodoo.

CEREMONIAL MAGICK

Ceremonial magick involves the use of ritualistic and ceremonial procedures and the invocation or evocation of spiritual entities or forces to achieve desired outcomes. Witches who practice ceremonial magick use symbols, sigils, astrological correspondences, and ritual tools such as candles, incense, wands, and robes. The witch may work with specific deities and entities on an ongoing basis and will make ritual offerings to these entities on her altar. In return, the witch receives the blessings and benefits of working with these deities and entities.

Goals of ceremonial magick can vary depending on the witch and her specific tradition, but common aims may include spiritual development, personal empowerment, manifestation of desires, communication with higher beings or realms, changing situations and conditions, and gaining access to valuable, hidden information.

THE 21 DIVISIONS

Also known as Dominican Vudú, The 21 Divisions is a syncretic magickal tradition that originated in the Dominican Republic. It combines elements of African, European, and Indigenous Caribbean spiritual practices and is referred to as a form of Afro-Caribbean or Afro-Latin spirituality. The 21 Divisions is focused on the veneration of certain spirits or lwa, which represent aspects of nature and human experience. The lwa are called upon for healing, protection, love, prosperity, and other requirements of living a physically and spiritually fulfilling life.

The tradition also incorporates elements of Catholicism, such as the veneration of saints, using Catholic prayers and icons in its rituals. The 21 Divisions tradition is characterized by its use of divination, which is performed using tools such as cards, shells, or stones. Divination is used to communicate with the lwa and to gain insight into one's personal life or future. I have always found The 21 Divisions to be an intriguing magickal practice.

ECLECTIC WITCHCRAFT

Eclectic witchcraft is a type of witchcraft that draws on the best of a variety of traditions and practices, integrating them in a personally meaningful way.

Eclecticism means to derive ideas, styles, or taste from a broad and diverse range of sources or styles. It refers to the practice of selecting or borrowing elements from varying sources with the intention of creating a perfectly tailored modus operandi. For the witch, an eclectic path derives from years of practice and the observation of outcomes and efficacy of a plethora of magickal systems and practices. By combining elements of these, the witch arrives at a blend *par excellence* of what would seem to be disparate constituents. Alchemy is the domain of this witch, who blends practices with acuity to arrive at precisely what she is aiming for. This witch uses the best of all magickal worlds rather than settling into any one tradition.

Eclectic witches incorporate practices and beliefs from Wicca, ceremonial magick, shamanism, herbalism, and even the world's religions. They don't stop at integrating spiritual practices. The eclectic witch, being the ultimate freedom purveyor, gathers her knowledge and practices from psychology, history, culture, and science. Unfettered yet informed, this witch has given herself permission to delve into and utilize any means at her disposal to create a self-satisfying and bespoke brand of magick.

There are many more magickal systems afforded to help today's witch align spiritually, mentally, emotionally, and physically with the perfect expression of self.

The path and practice of the witch are fluid and self-initiating, marked with freedom and defined by power. The witch is free to choose any magickal system desired to fit the ends, knowing that skill level, experience, and constitution are important considerations. While some witches may invoke or evoke spirits as part of their practice, other witches craft their strongest magick with plants and herbs. Each witch is a unique event on the screen of consciousness. Fully Divine and fully empowered, the witch chooses for herself which magickal practices she will engage, and why. The longer a witch practices magick and witchcraft, the more her experience deepens, her senses heighten, her gifts are perfected, and her ability to solve more complex issues and a wider range of human conditions expands. As this happens, the witch grows into an even more formidable agent of creation, transformation, and destruction.

THE WITCH'S APOTHECARY

———•———•———•———

The plant kingdom nourishes a witch's practice, from planting, growing, and nurturing to harvesting and employing these potent healers. The witch reveres plants as the bounty of the Goddess in the natural world. Plants have long been integrated and gently laced through a witch's practice and spirituality as well as her service to others who are hurting, have lost their way, or have a happy occasion unfolding, such as the birth of a baby. In any circumstance, there are plants who can help, and these are to be found in the palms and pockets of the most powerful witches walking the planet.

In my kitchen are a collection of herbs tightly sealed in glass jars from as far away as Egypt and as close to home as the wild basil pushing itself up through the cracks of my patio pavement, a holdover from a former garden that I've grown to love and harvest. In other cork-topped glass jars are herbs with olive oil added to them to produce energized healing, cleansing, and attraction. These are oils that I'll use in my rituals and spellwork and share with others.

An apothecary can serve as a witch's physical portal to plant spirits. Though the apothecary in a modern context may recall visions of a pharmacy, the origins harken back to ancient Egypt, Greece, and Rome, where apothecaries were dispensaries for preparations and remedies made from plants by skilled healers. The witch and the ancients have a common understanding in healing with plants: they know plants serve as gateways and can work in tandem with other energies, including deities, astrological influences, and elements.

Shamans, herbalists, chemists, farmers, and gardeners have all experienced aspects of the magickal nature of plants.

This is the witch's experience with and of plants. The witch holds all nature as a sacred representation of the Divine, or the Great Invisible Spirit. To some, this is God and/or Goddess. To others, it is the quantum field. Energy is real, and it is all that is real. The entire third dimension is a construct of sorts, and a representation of worlds beyond. Plants can usher us into the greater world beyond this one.

Witches use plants to amplify spiritual practice and help those who are seeking mental, emotional, physical, and even spiritual healing. Humanity has accumulated an array of means to become imbalanced in body and mind, which can be especially felt in the technologically advanced cultures whose people rarely engage nature on its terms. Plants enable us to undo misalignment and recalibrate the body, mind, and spirit to harmony.

The Japanese practice of *shinrin-yoku* involves immersing oneself in nature by spending time in a forest or other natural environment, without mobile phones or any technology. This "forest bathing" was developed in Japan in the 1980s to promote health and well-being by reconnecting humans with nature. Far from being a simple walk in the woods, which would do worlds of good for many of us, forest bathing is an intentional practice of engaging with nature through the senses... taking off one's shoes to feel the cool, dirt-covered earth below, drawing in a deep breath and smelling the fragrance of trees swirled with flowers, and feeling the warm sunlight on the skin as it pierces leaves and branches. This is total immersion in nature for the ultimate healing, witch style.

We find the cottage witch or green witch in a perpetual forest bath, in nature, plucking seeds, leaves, and flowers from here and there and scavenging roots and shoots from the forest floor for the next healing ingredient in a tea or tincture, or salve.

PLANTS

In her aspect as healer, the witch knows plants are an irreplaceable and indispensable ally in many areas.

HEALING

The witch uses plants not only for their medicinal properties, which green witches have learned meticulously over decades, but also to aid with emotional and spiritual ailments. No one can deny the calming effect of a cup of chamomile tea at the end of a long day, or the fragrant aroma of lavender added to a natural soap that invites us into a warm bath and unwinds taut muscles.

WITCHCRAFT & MAGICK

Plants are used to create spells, charms, and potions. Each plant carries unique magickal properties and can be used to create different effects or achieve specific goals. Rosemary and the sages—including blue, white, and clary sage—are used for space clearing, purification, or protection, while plants like lavender or rose are used for relaxation or rituals and spell work involving love and relationships.

DIVINATION

The witch turns to mugwort, frankincense, and bay leaves for use in divination, such as scrying or reading Tarot. These power agents enhance intuition and psychic abilities, as well as visions and dreams.

SPIRITUAL CONNECTION

Many witches use plants to connect with nature and the spiritual realm. Plants are believed to have their own spirit or energy and can be used in rituals or ceremonies to honor the natural world and to connect with the Divine.

CLEANSING AND CLEARING SPACES

The witch turns to sage as an ally for cleansing, clearing, and protecting spaces from negative energies. The mighty sage comes in a plethora of varieties and serves medicinal (anti-inflammatory and antiseptic) and spiritual (purification and protection) purposes, which is why it is dearly loved by the witch. Blue sage, clary sage, white sage, or black sage can be burned in a bundle that produces a thick smoke sufficient to clear the energy of any room or space, leaving behind only freshness.

TEAS

The witch uses plants to heal in the form of teas, tinctures, salves, poultices, liniments, and even soaps and candles.

When I was a little girl under the watchful eye of my witch mother, the slightest issue in the body temple would elicit healing remedies from the plant kingdom. A sour stomach was solved with a cup of hot goldenseal with a tad of honey added, though the honey did precious little to conceal the strong taste of the herb, which repulsed me as a child. I did not know then what I know now.

Goldenseal is a master healer that can provide:

Immune system support: Goldenseal contains the compounds berberine and hydrastine, which have immune-boosting properties, helping the body fight infections and illnesses. This made it a favorite of my mother for colds and flu as well.

Digestive health: Goldenseal can improve digestion, relieve constipation and diarrhea, and reduce inflammation in the digestive tract.

Skin health: The berberine in goldenseal has antibacterial and anti-inflammatory properties that can help with skin conditions, including acne and eczema.

Anti-inflammatory effects: Goldenseal contains alkaloids that have anti-inflammatory properties to soothe inflammation in the body that accompany ailments such as arthritis, allergies, and respiratory infections.

Blood sugar control: Some studies suggest that the compound berberine found in goldenseal can help improve insulin sensitivity and blood sugar control in people with Type 2 diabetes.

Peppermint is another popular herbal tea loved by the witch that has been used traditionally for both health and spiritual purposes.

Digestive health: Due to its antispasmodic properties, peppermint tea can relieve digestive concerns like indigestion, bloating, and gas and help relax the muscles in the digestive tract, improving digestion.

Respiratory health: A good strong whiff of peppermint tea can help relieve respiratory issues, including stuffy nose, coughs, and sinus congestion. Thanks to its strong anti-inflammatory and antiviral properties, it also can help fend off infections.

Dental health: Peppermint tea can help improve dental health by reducing bacteria in the mouth and freshening breath. In the mornings, I practice an Ayurvedic morning ritual called oil pulling, in which coconut oil is pulled back and forth through the teeth for several minutes, ridding the gums and spaces in between the teeth of dangerous overgrowth of bacteria. I add a few drops of peppermint to the oil, and the invigorating and clean feeling in my mouth is unparalleled.

Chamomile is a favorite of witches for when rest and relaxation are needed.

Improved sleep: Chamomile tea is known for its calming properties and helps improve sleep quality and reduce insomnia.

Reduced inflammation: Chamomile tea is also an anti-inflammatory agent that reduces inflammation in the body and can therefore help to relieve pain from ailments that are caused by inflammation, especially arthritis.

Digestive health: Chamomile tea has been used for centuries to relieve digestive issues, calming and soothing the entire digestive tract.

Anxiety relief: Chamomile tea has a calming effect on the body, mind, and spirit and may help reduce symptoms of anxiety and depression.

Ginger is a potent healer. I always keep it in my cupboard for:

Digestive health: Also containing anti-inflammatory and antispasmodic properties, ginger tea relieves digestive issues and sour stomach.

Immune system boost: Ginger tea helps boost the immune system due to its high levels of antioxidants. My mother counted on these when administering hot ginger tea to us with onion, honey, and lemon added.

Respiratory health: Given ginger tea's anti-inflammatory and anti-viral properties, it can help relieve symptoms of respiratory issues, including coughs, colds, and other viral infections.

Menstrual cramp relief: Ginger tea has pain-relieving and relaxation properties that can even relieve menstrual cramps.

After a long day, it's not unusual for me to settle in with a nice, hot cup of ginger tea, one of my personal favorites, with a bit of agave nectar added. I put my feet up and allow ginger's soothing, healing properties to take effect, and it never fails me.

Other mainstay teas for healing, relaxation, spiritual upliftment, mood boosting, and immune support are black, red, white, and green teas as well as lemon balm, spearmint, stinging nettle, rosehip, and echinacea, another of my mother's favorites. In the flower tea family, hibiscus, currently in my kitchen, can be used for blood pressure and cholesterol management, and liver health. While in China, I fell in love with chrysanthemum tea and bought a canister of the yellow buds home to steep in hot water and sip on, knowing that the tea helps to support healthy eyes.

Innumerable benefits from teas are accessible to all. Teas are simple to prepare, making them the perfect healing remedies for witches to recommend to those seeking aid.

TINCTURES

Witches create tinctures with herbs and other plants by covering them with vodka, vinegar, or alcohol, and tightly sealing them in a glass container for seven to fourteen days. The tinctures last for years if kept in a cool, dry cupboard, out of the glaring rays of the sun. They can work their healing magick with as little as one to two drops under the tongue.

Tinctures are tiny, concentrated doses of healing remedy because the vodka, vinegar, or alcohol extracts the active compounds in the plant, making these bio-available and safe for adults. Because of their potency, only a drop or two is required; a tincture prepared by a witch for a client tends to last for quite a while.

SALVES, POULTICES, AND LINIMENTS

If there are topical issues ailing the client of a witch, this family of remedies can bring about almost instant relief. A salve, poultice, and liniment are all topical preparations, yet are different in form, texture, and application method.

SALVE

A salve is a semi-solid ointment that is applied topically to the skin. We make a salve with herbal extracts, oils, and beeswax, which are melted together and then cooled to form a solid or semi-solid consistency. Salves are used to moisturize and protect the skin as well as to provide relief from minor skin irritations and injuries such as cuts, bruises, and insect bites. I've also seen salves used as beauty treatments. I use a salve whose active ingredient is aloe vera gel harvested from my aloe plant. This salve is for slathering generously on the face for moisturizing, relief of skin irritations, clearing clogged pores, exfoliation, and treating sunburn.

POULTICE

A poultice is a soft, moist mass of herbal or other natural materials that is applied directly to the skin to provide relief from pain, inflammation, and even cuts and bruises, if the herbs and plant material are not the stinging kind. Poultices are typically made by crushing or grinding fresh or dried herbs, leaves, flowers, or roots, and then mixing them with a liquid such as water, oil, or vinegar to form a paste-like consistency. The poultice is then applied to the affected area and covered with a bandage or cloth to hold it in place. My grandmother was keen on these types of treatments, as they were easy to whip up in her kitchen and she could tie them in place on us as kids, without us having to be bedridden. The plant medicine was silently at work as we kept on about the business of a child's life.

LINIMENT

A liniment is a liquid preparation that is applied topically to the skin to provide relief from pain, stiffness, bruises, sprains, and injuries. Liniments are made by combining herbal extracts or essential oils with a base of alcohol, vinegar, or oil, which is then applied to the affected area using a cotton ball, cloth, or spray bottle. Liniments can also be used on the chest when congestion prevents a good night's sleep. Eucalyptus, tea tree, and rosemary all open the airways quite nicely when added to an oil and rubbed on the chest.

Whether administering a tea or a salve, poultice, or liniment, the witch as healer has a commanding understanding of the properties of each plant and its effects, not just physically, but reaching all the way into the spirit realm.

This occult knowledge of plants, herbs, trees, roots, vegetables, fruits, and the bounty of nature afford the witch enhanced capabilities for healing and correcting as she tends to forests, glens, and gardens. I carefully and intentionally select herbs and nature's offerings from all over the world for specific uses—from the famed spice markets of Aswan, Egypt, prized by magicians for their rare herbs called for in rituals and spell work, to the aloe and basil I grow myself. My apothecary is a rich demonstration of the plant kingdom's ability to serve as a portal to worlds beyond based on energetic correspondences.

A visit to any magick shoppe or witchcraft emporium will highlight a simple yet poignant truth: The green in every witch knows there's a tree or plant, root, or shoot for anything that ails the human condition, and the witch is ready to use them.

THE WITCH'S CODE

———•———•———•———

*T*here is a code of the witch referred to as The Witches Pyramid, a four-level edifice with each level corresponding to a statement of action that guides the witch. These four guiding principles of magick are:

To Know
To Will
To Dare
To Keep Silent

Examining each of these spheres yields occult knowledge about how a witch comports herself.

To know requires study, application, and experimentation. A powerful witch studies nature, books, and people, then marries that information with practical application of knowledge for outcomes in the physical world that garner wisdom. A witch who knows the wind as an aspect of the air element has sat in the wood, quiet and still, attuned to the wind wafting across her skin, raising hairs as it goes, whispering in her ear, blowing through her hair, and lifting her spirits. The witch who studies the element of air knows the wind.

A powerful witch garners this knowledge not merely from reading books or filling up with information found online. A witch's knowing crosses the bounds of the physical plane and enters realms beyond the conscious mind. To know is to be at one with the infinite field from which all information is sourced.

To will is to have one's solar plexus aligned and to hold a clear intention in all one's working and magickal practices. To will is to intend, to move in the direction chosen, and to persist in that direction until the outcome has been firmly established. Nothing monumental can be created on the third-dimensional plane without an absolute, rock-solid will that surmounts all obstacles to achieve the desired result.

The witch, being her own empowered being, does not rely on anyone or anything else. Therefore, the witch's will is rooted in the infinite power of our ancient archetype and the primordial forces that have existed before time and space.

To dare is to be courageous. Courage is not the absence of fear but the power to move forward confidently in the face of fear. The witch dares to be great, dares to commune with otherworldly spirits, and dares to exercise the will for desired outcomes, no matter what others may think, say, or do. A witch is daring.

To keep silent is to be a crypt for secrets that are not to be revealed to the unready, the unwise, the unlearned, and in many cases, the uninitiated. A witch knows how to keep a secret, or even many. Part of being a witch is understanding the deep, inner secrets and mysteries of nature and one's craft, and to be a keeper of these secrets, no matter what situation may arise. An aspect of holding a secret is that no one knows that you are holding a secret. A witch's silence protects the witch, the coven the witch may belong to, and the unlearned, unprepared, or unready.

The witch is born of darkness. Thus, secrets are natural and part of her occult persona. A witch who cannot keep secrets will not be entrusted with those matters that rule the cycles of birth, life and death, the rhythm of our cosmos, the elements, the inner workings of magick, and the ancient mysteries.

A fervid commitment to the witch's code may lead to initiation.

INITIATION

Once the archetype of the witch is engaged, the relationship deepens. We open more to living as a witch in the natural world and commit to making our entire lives magickal. Dormant energies awaken, and as they do, power is unleashed. As this process unfolds, which may take years or even decades, the one who has chosen to outwardly live as a witch may undertake formal training and initiation.

Initiation as a witch takes many forms and can vary from witch to witch, or from tradition to tradition for witches who practice in a coven of a specific tradition. An initiation enters the witch—even one who is solitary—into a secret universal coven of sorts where deeper mysteries are revealed. The witch is an archetype expressed through witches who walk the earth. During initiation, the witch offers devotion, even as we are devoted to our gods and goddesses and to our children and lovers. The promise of devotion means commitment to this way of being and to all it entails. The path is not always easy for a witch; we take a vow so that we will stay the course, even when the road is rocky.

When a witch is initiated, it will be secretive and only occur after intensive training, years of study, coven practice, or solitary practice. The initiation is a universal event and affair involving not just the witch but her Divine counterparts in spirit realms as well.

The witch does not work alone but is forever in union and communion with nature and the spirit world—including the realms of the dead—and with cosmic forces including lunar, solar, and stellar influences. This channel of communion with energies and entities beyond the third dimension is opened, established, and maintained by study, magickal practice, sacred observances, and a ritualistic approach to all aspects of life. As a witch grows in this communion, there will be an urge from the archetype to be initiated into the magickal arts and sciences as a willing, ready, and well-prepared practitioner who can work on behalf of others because of her immense spiritual power.

Witches have access to an infinite well of pure power that can be used in any way one desires, according to intention and will. When the intention, will, words, and actions are married to the corresponding elements and ingredients, and the action is performed at the appropriate time, changes in one's inner world and its outer manifestation are catalyzed.

Initiation opens the door to deeper wisdom and understanding in a never-ending cycle of mastery which is forever expanding the witch's use of power in the realm of humans. The more the witch delves deeper into study, practice, and ritual, the more the witch can affect powerful magick. These feed each other in a never-ending wheel of perfection.

Initiation begets the cycle.

In our tradition, initiation occurs on the winter solstice in a ritual that includes an oath from the initiate, a new name for the initiate, and the passing on of potent magickal energies in an unbroken current from those who were initiated before. In this regard, newly initiated witches become custodians and gatekeepers of both the secrets and energetic flame of magick, which they, too, may pass forward one day.

Though I have experienced several initiations, my first initiation into witchcraft was a solitary affair in which, after years of study and releasing old religious programming, I dedicated myself to the practice of the craft. I vowed to live a magickal life as a witch and to honor and live by the witch's code. I gained a new name, one that was a magickal moniker for quite some time until I gained another name in an advanced initiation, years later. My first initiation remains one of the high points of my life because of my decision to tap into the power of the witch.

A witch decides to live a magickal life. This doesn't occur by happenstance. It requires a premeditated act of will to align with the witch's code, receive training, and be initiated into a lifetime of ritual and magickal practice. Such a decision and commitment changes the fabric of one's consciousness. Initiation is rightly celebrated by all concerned, especially the coven. When a new witch has emerged from the primordial forces of magick, it is an epic event. Once initiation occurs, life will never be the same, as is immediately apparent even during the initiatory rites.

This life decision, no less monumental in nature than deciding to have children or choosing a life partner, is one that will fuel the witch's practice and the witch herself through the certain tribulations of life, while exalting her to the rarified air of those who harbor the mysteries.

THE SPHERE OF SPIRITS

———●———●———●———

Witches commune with a plethora of spirits. In the witch's paradigm, spirits can be powerful allies. To determine spirits with which to commune and cooperate, the witch uses intuition, divination, deep knowledge of the spirit world from personal experience, and generational information passed through lineage and tradition—and, of course, the spirits themselves.

Before we can comprehend the spirit world witches operate in, it's important to understand more about the nature of reality and dimensions of consciousness. Taking a multi-disciplinary approach to the witch and her world—from the fields of psychology and the witch as archetype to astrological confluences, to scientific discovery including quantum physics—allows us to broaden and deepen our understanding of this enigmatic figure who often eludes accurate understanding.

The field of quantum physics enthuses me as a witch because it speaks the language of the soul and spirit. Quantum theory can help us understand magickal practices of the witch that may appear strange yet have always proven efficacious. What underpins the practices of the witch? What makes them effective? What about the nature of reality?

THE NATURE OF REALITY AND CONSCIOUS AGENTS

The field of quantum physics has made great strides in helping us understand the nature of reality by means of scientific experimentation, yielding often shocking results. Though science alone cannot explain the nature of reality, it can be an enlightening guide.

Scientific breakthroughs can afford us the opportunity to finally meet the witch where she has stood for eons: in the liminal space between worlds.

We follow quantum physics and researchers in the field closely, as it aligns with what we practice in spirituality, magick, and witchcraft. One of the problems science seeks to solve, in this field and in others, is the "hard problem of consciousness." It cannot be proven that matter arises from consciousness, yet this is what many scientists believe, even without hard evidence. This is also the mind-body problem of proving just how the mind affects the body.

One of my favorite scientific researchers on the subject is neuroscientist Donald Hoffman, Ph.D., professor in the Department of Cognitive Sciences at the University of California, Irvine, with joint appointments in the Department of Philosophy, the Department of Logic and Philosophy of Science, and the School of Computer Science.

Professor Hoffman has proposed a bold theory—that objects do not exist independently of us perceiving them and that all that really exists are conscious agents.

Bold as it may be, this aligns, to the letter, with a witch's paradigm of the universe, which is why I mention it here. Professor Hoffman goes on to elaborate in his book *The Case Against Reality* that space/time is a construct and is not fundamental to reality. Consciousness is fundamental, underpinning all reality, from which, as Professor Hoffman would refer to them, conscious agents emerge.

In witch parlance, conscious agents would be spirits.

You can imagine why I find the decades-long work of Professor Hoffman so fascinating. He and kindred scientific researchers who are ziplining past constraints in the fields of neuroscience, quantum mechanics, and psychology are now proposing answers to questions about consciousness that have been debated over for centuries.

We now have reports from science that agree with the witch's knowing, as the Nobel Prize winners in physics for 2022 have shown us: the universe is not *locally real*. What does that mean? *Real* in this context means that independent objects have definite properties independent of observation, and *local* means that objects can only be influenced by their surroundings, and that influence cannot travel faster than the speed of light.

We now know that these statements cannot both be true. The evidence points to mind-boggling concepts. One, that objects do not have definite properties, such as shape and form, before being observed and measured; and second, that objects are solely influenced by their surroundings. Without going too far into the thicket of human consciousness, quantum mechanics, or the theory of entanglement, I can share three factors salient to the witch, magick, and witchcraft, and why they work:

- When we are not observing or measuring an object in third-dimensional reality, does it exist? Evidence proves it does not.
- Objects are acted upon by factors beyond the immediate surroundings.
- Reality is not what we may have been taught it is, or previously believed.

Professor Hoffman has proven by mathematical equations that the likelihood that we are perceiving reality with our five senses is exactly zero.

This begs the questions: What is reality? How is it perceived? And how do we know if, or when, we are perceiving reality with accuracy?

The answers are shocking. We are not perceiving reality with our five senses. Space/time is not real, nor is it fundamental to reality. Consciousness is fundamental, and, if Professor Hoffman's Conscious Realism Theory is correct, the real world consists solely of conscious agents.

When I study quantum physics, it's a smoking gun for me as a witch. This body of thought gives a framework explaining why our spells and charms work. The theory of entanglement explains why sympathetic magick works. Sympathetic magick depends upon the laws of the universe. We now understand that particles that were once entangled are always entangled.

This is an energy conversation that reveals the hidden layers of the witch's connection to energy, the spirit world, and consciousness itself.

THE LIMINAL SPACE BETWEEN WORLDS

Liminal means to occupy a space or position on both sides of a boundary or threshold. The liminal space is the basis for witches being known as "hedge-riders." In the physical dimension, the hedge circled a town outside of which was the witch's hut, deep in an enchanted wood. The witch didn't live in town. She visited the town when people required her services. The town represented the third dimension of consciousness, where we play out the human drama.

The witch lived deep in the enchanted wood, surrounded by nature spirits humming their song in the wind, trees, stream, and stone.

The figurative hedge is a dividing line, a crossover point, and a threshold. It provides protection for the unaware, untrained, and uninitiated in the ways of navigating worlds beyond. The liminal space is the witch's natural abode, as if having her right foot in third dimensional reality and her left in the infinite dimensions of consciousness beyond. Dancing in the liminal brings the best of both domains of consciousness to the center point within a witch, where they create a convergence of power and potentiality.

With the town as a symbol of the mundane world, and the enchanted wood as a symbol of the magickal worlds beyond, the hedge is a blurry line the witch can ride for the benefit of both sides.

SPIRITS

Spirits who are not flesh and blood reside in dimensions beyond and could be referred to as *conscious agents* to use Professor Hoffman's verbology. For the witch, spirits are prevalent, and our communication with them is an integral part of our craft and way of being.

Whether the spirits are called higher self, gods and goddesses, enlightened ancestors, spirit guides, angels, archangels, ascended masters, and many more spirits than we can identify and name, what we know is this: An immense spiritual world exists, of which our physical dimension is but a tiny portion. A great majority of existence is imperceptible to the five senses. It is this majority that we will discuss here.

While the five senses do not perceive beyond this physical realm, the extrasensory abilities of the witch do. From psychic knowledge to clairvoyance, the witch calls upon these abilities to commune with spirits.

Some suggest that a map of the cosmos would be triple layered, to include celestial spirits, terrestrial spirits, and infernal spirits. I would suggest that maps are aids in understanding and are not set in stone. A map can change, offering a differing view of the territory.

If we utilize this three-tiered map of the cosmos, we understand that each layer contains countless dimensions of consciousness, from the lowest vibration to the highest and everything in between. This is also the case in the world of humans. There are no inherently good or not-good spirits, and there are no useless spirits. If a spirit exists, it exists for a reason. Purpose is encoded in existence. The two are inseparable.

Since there are no inherently good or malevolent spirits, and every spirit has a purpose, then there is never a need for a witch to be in fear of any spirit. This understanding helps a witch be courageous, as one must be to interact with the spirit world on an intentional basis.

CELESTIAL REALM

Exploring the realms of spirits gives us a glimpse into the world of the witch, who she communes with, why, and with what outcomes.

The celestial realm consists of spirits that vibrate at higher frequencies and are benevolent or helpful, such as archangels and angels, and gods and goddesses. Others include:

HIGHER SELF

The higher self is the true self, beyond the human self. It knows all, sees all, and is infinite. In the parlance of Professor Hoffman, it may well be a conscious agent.

The true self guides this incarnation and evolves and ascends us in the practice of magick and the craft.

ENLIGHTENED ANCESTORS

Our original ancestor is Source, from which all our forebears flow. Our ancestors form an unbroken connection to Source. As we become ancestors, we continue the flow forward.

There are different types of ancestors, just as there are a vast array of entities and spirits on the other side of the veil. It's important to understand who we are contacting.

For my personal practice, I've chosen to commune with enlightened ancestors whom I know have a vested interest in my evolution. Our ancestors continue to ascend as we honor and connect with them. They are committed to their own ascension as well as ours, due to the nature of the entire ancestral line: it is connected. We all go up together, as if linked by soul cords.

Crossed-over spirits are of a vast variety. Some are lost. Some are reluctant to return to Source. Some are caught up in the astral plane. Some have unfinished business here and continue to roam, seeking closure. Some don't know they're dead yet.

Wisdom, training, study, and practice are essential when discerning spirits. Further, we ought to be discerning in our dealings with all spirits.

SPIRIT GUIDES

Spirit Guides are helpful beings who may not have completed their own ascension journey yet are willing to help us with ours. They may have been teachers in the third dimension for humanity. Developing close kinship with spirit guides put us in a partnership, similar to the ancestral partnership, where all parties are committed to their own growth and are unified in intention. This facilitates ascension. If you're intuitive, you may be in touch with many spirit guides.

ASCENDED MASTERS

Ascended masters are souls who have passed through the veil after an incarnation of reaching the highest levels of initiation and are now committed to helping all evolve. Ascended masters can be approached and communed with by all, if one is willing to persist in meditative practices that thin the veil.

Like spirit guides, yet more universal in scope and power, the ascended masters take on cosmic duties for the ascension of humanity.

TERRESTRIAL REALM

Nature spirits have been acknowledged and worked with (or against) in every culture of humanity, in every age. There is no denying their existence, without denying the experience of all cultures in nature. I have witnessed many inexplicable wonders in nature that I can only credit to nature spirits. You may have had similar experiences.

TERRESTRIAL SPIRITS

Terrestrial spirits are those closest to us in spirit realms, including elemental and nature spirits both mythic and energetic:

- Earth: gnomes, elves, trolls, dwarfs
- Air: fairies, sylphs, pixies, sprites (although some sprites are water sprites)
- Fire: phoenix, salamanders, dragons
- Water: merpeople, undines/nymphs, sirens

Our ancestors were immersed in nature, without the distractions that inundate us today. They were completely enveloped in the river and its sounds, smells, and spray. They experienced all of nature as Divine and had deemed this truth so imperative to their daily mode of operation that they invented a mythological language for it.

From the periodical *Theosophical Siftings*, Volume 1:

> "The creatures evolved in the four kingdoms of earth, air, fire, and water, and called by the Kabbalists gnomes, sylphs, salamanders, and undines. They may be termed the forces of nature, and will either

operate as the servile agents of general law, or may be employed by the disembodied spirits — whether pure or impure — and by living adepts of magic and sorcery, to produce desired phenomenal results. Such beings never become men."

HOUSE AND LAND SPIRITS

- Spirits who dwell on the land where a home, building, or other residence may be.
- Spirits of those who may have lived and died in a home prior to the current occupants.

INFERNAL REALM

The infernal realm is the habitation of fallen spirits and low vibration entities and thought forms. The infernal realm is not situated beneath the earth, yet we refer to it as down because of its lower vibration.

THE WITCH AS KEEPER OF COSMIC ORDER

Witches maintain cosmic order. This includes working with spirits. We tend to the order of the dimensions, seen and unseen. We can detect spirits, and if these spirits are not where they're supposed to be in the grand scheme of cosmic order, we're empowered to do something about it because we know we are Divine and an infinite power is forever at our disposal.

As witches, we are emissaries who travel between the dimensions at will. We are the midwife and the death doula. At the crossroads you will find us, and in the liminal space between worlds, where communing with spirits is natural.

INTIMATE VISCERAL CONNECTION

Spirit connection and communion is strengthened and facilitated by the witch's actions, habits, offerings, and rituals. A witch who cultivates a relationship with a particular spirit or family of spirits is arming herself with the ability to call on entities who have a different perspective and different problem-solving abilities than the witch herself. We could call a witch's cadre of spirits her "spiritual board of directors." These bonds are fortified through:

INTENTION

The witch is intentional about which spirits she is in communion with, and why. Influencing this intentional choice may be the magickal or witchcraft tradition the witch is part of; her culture and ancestry; her training and proficiency; and of course, the outcomes the witch is desirous of catalyzing.

PRACTICE

A witch develops a practice of speaking with spirits, listening to spirits, having lunch and drinks with spirits, setting a plate out for ancestral spirits, buying flowers and gifts for spirits, and giving offerings in alignment with each spirit. As with relationships in the physical realm, spirit relationships are fostered and deepened through connection, communion, and reciprocity.

RITUALS

A witch practices rituals to connect with the spirit realm, one of which is the *Dumb Supper*, a meal conducted in complete silence. It is a dinner prepared and eaten with the spirits of the ancestors and loved ones who have crossed over. This séance-style feast is usually conducted on All Hallow's Eve, otherwise known as Halloween. It is interesting to note that the following day, November 1, is All Saints Day, in which Catholics honor saints who have passed on, and the day after that is All Souls Day, in which prayers ascend for those who have passed on. These disparate customs and the attendant rituals are connected through their desire and intention to connect the world of the living with the world of the dead.

HOW SPIRITS COMMUNICATE

Everyone is a spiritual being. Spirit communication is intentionally pursued and pulled to the forefront of the witch's awareness for palpable connection with the spirit world and powerful allies.

Spirits communicate energetically. They transmit messages into our conscious awareness by a myriad of means:

- An intuitive sense of *yes!*
- A sense of foreboding
- Tingling
- Symbols seen repeatedly
- Bodily temperature fluctuations: cold/heat
- Body functions: sweating, faster heartbeat, hairs standing up
- A sense that some is standing behind you, or next to you, or seated on the bed
- Instantaneous knowing: knowing things without knowing how you know them; knowing information without a thought process or deduction
- Visions and dreams
- Sparkles above one's head or in one's line of sight
- Books falling off the shelf at you
- Items appearing and/or disappearing
- Hummingbird(s) at your window
- Dragonflies and butterflies landing on you or coming unusually close

Spirits don't speak a human language, so it is the extrasensory perceptions of the witch that make it possible to ascertain messages from the spirit world and make sense of them for practical application. Intuition and divination are helpful in spirit communication. Intuition is honed over time through a devoted, unwavering, and committed practice of meditation. Divination can be used to determine the nature of spirits a witch may encounter, how to respond, and the protocols for interaction.

Interaction with the spirit world is everyone's right and the witch's habit. We may have all experienced the touch of an ancestral spirit or the guiding hand of an angel or an animal spirit delivering a profound message. These are all natural interactions with the spirit world.

Witches choose which spirits to interact with, including gods and goddesses, ancestors, ascended masters, and others, to seek wisdom, gain allies, and move mountains on the physical plane.

GRIMOIRE OR BOOK OF SHADOWS

———•———•———•———

*F*or the practicing witch, a *grimoire*—or Book of Shadows—is vital.

The word grimoire is from the French word *grammaire*, which at one time referred to all books written in Latin. Over time, the word morphed to refer to a book of spells, incantations, rituals, readings, correspondences, and all else the witch deems important enough to preserve in a written record.

The Book of Shadows was pioneered by Gerald Gardner, who could be considered the father of Wicca, in the early 20th century. This book contained rituals, spells, and information used by a *coven*— a group of witches who practice together in a tightly bonded unit that is held to secrecy concerning some or most of the rituals and practices. The Book of Shadows became such a staple that it moved beyond Wicca to both solitary witches and secular witches, who adopted the term and usage.

Many now view a grimoire and a Book of Shadows as one and the same, though definitions, practical use, and customs of humanity shift over time, taking with it all we utilize. Everything morphs. The witch understands this truth and avails herself of potent magickal practices and items that are worth adopting and integrating into her practice.

Once the grimoire or Book of Shadows is created, it is deemed to have a magickal or talismanic power of its own, due to its intended use, its consecration into the magickal arts, and its contents. These charged magickal books are hidden or kept out of reach of the uninformed, uninitiated, and unready. In some traditions, a witch's grimoire is destroyed after her death. In others, a grimoire can be passed on after the demise of its creator but must first be subjected to layers of energetic "locking" as well as a physical wrapping, to assure accessibility is reserved for the new owner.

Some witches use a journal or notebook. While this is not a formal grimoire or Book of Shadows, it serves as a handy place to keep notes and ideas. It might include the feelings one experiences while practicing magick and honoring the rituals throughout the year, or other personal expressions one is inspired to write down.

Over many years of practicing witchcraft and magick, I've accumulated several magickal journals and a few grimoires. While my magickal journals are plentiful, I have four grimoires, each dedicated to specific practices that are important to me.

I started my first and original grimoire on April 24, 2006 after many years of studying witchcraft and magick, when I came to the realization that I'd been practicing these all my life, and so had my forebears. This grimoire contains my magickal name from my first initiation; the names of the four archangels I work with as a Christian Witch, along with their correspondences; hand-drawn runes and their meanings; full-moon rituals; a ritual titled Leaping Into a New Spiritual Identity (see Part 3); my magickal motto; prayers; and a list of magick books I've read or would love to read.

Another of my grimoires is devoted to the Goddess in all her manifold expressions. It contains the names of goddesses I work with and their splendid titles; important notes from H.P. Blavatsky and Eliphas Levi, both giants in the world of occult studies; and all rituals relating to the Goddess, with odes specifically to Isis and Inanna. I am devoted to and have relationships with these two goddesses.

Another of my grimoires is for Kabbalistic Magick and contains penetrating notes and secrets of the Tree of Life, the archangels that rule each of the ten spheres on the Tree, and the legions of angels each of these commands. Because this grimoire is dedicated to Jewish mysticism and magick, it contains verses from the Hebrew Bible and their application in rituals and spells.

The final and largest grimoire I'll speak of here is a giant, green, leatherbound book from a magick store in New Orleans. It has a clasp on the front and is reminiscent of the Book of Shadows in the popular television show *Charmed*. While many elements of pop culture's television shows and movies on magick and witchcraft are not accurate, other elements are based on truths in the witch's world. This grimoire contains the names and properties of deities I work with, sigils, spells, and herbs and their magickal uses. It also includes the names of angels and the issues they help with and how to summon each.

The big book of magick is real. A witch keeps a handwritten record of the most important aspects of the magick and witchcraft she practices, along with reference material germane to each spell or to the outcomes of a certain set of spells. Thus our rituals, magickal workings, spells, incantations, and prayers become more powerful over time, the more they are referenced, utilized, and perfected.

Evolution as a witch is required. To ever stretch forward, onward, and upward, one must give careful attention to past mistakes to be sure not to repeat them, while also considering successes and how these were created, step by step. Taking notes elevates and evolves the witch and her practice.

The grimoire or Book of Shadows is a written evolutionary ladder the witch ascends to ever more powerful magick. As I gaze at older entries in my grimoires, I behold a younger witch finding her way, and I smile at the changes that have occurred over time that might have been missed were I not carefully chronicling them. The witch honors her path and magick by registering these in one of the most powerful agents available to the witch: words.

Now we give attention to stories from witches who have documented their path and are courageously willing to share sacred pages from their archives with us.

PART TWO

Divine Alignments with the Primordial Energies of Magick and Cycles of Nature

The witch is a person who understands the interconnectedness of all things, and who seeks to live in harmony with the natural world.

— SCOTT CUNNINGHAM

YOU'RE A WITCH!

It happened in the parking lot of my daughter's school. I had just dropped her off to her first-grade class and, as I returned to my vehicle, I met up with another mom who was taking her tiny tot inside. On this fall day, which is still seared in my memory, I was wearing a black hat that I absolutely loved. As the other mom and I had a quick exchange of small talk on the parking lot, her son looked up at me, raised his forefinger to point directly at my face, and exclaimed, "You're a witch!"

His tone was not mean—it was fascinated. He saw me. He *knew* me.

This was during a period in my life when I was still hiding my Tarot deck in its bag, further carefully wrapped in gorgeous and colorful cloth and tucked away in a drawer under clothes so my Baptist husband wouldn't discover my "heresy."

The boy's mother was instantly horrified, turning to him abruptly and chiding him with "Don't say that! What's wrong with you?"

The boy looked confused, having no idea what he'd done that was so wrong.

Mom turned her flustered attention back to me and apologized profusely. "I don't know what got into him!"

But I knew exactly what had "gotten into him." Divinity. He had read my soul in an instant. I was hiding, and he called me out. Children that young have yet to learn how to spin a lie, so his words were pure and true, as was the energy behind them.

We ended our brief, yet poignant, three-way encounter in a huff, with the other mom still irritated. I climbed into my car and sat there, dazed. I needed a minute to digest. Ruminate. Let it percolate. That little boy's three words stayed with me all day and the day after—and in fact, all the way up to this very day.

Kids *know*. He had exposed the secrets I was attempting to keep hidden. Kids are intuitive. They know far more than we think they do. I was uncomfortable with a little boy reading me like a book while his mother— standing eye-to-eye with me—didn't see what he saw. My clever disguise of being a normal human was working on the mother. I couldn't get it past her son.

What struck me is that his words were spoken with no malice or ill intent. He looked at me as if he were looking at a Disney movie. He meant no harm by anything he said. He was simply making a statement of fact, with none of the heat his mother had attached to it.

How was it that a little boy could be so comfortable with the idea of me being a witch, and even fascinated by the idea, while I still struggled under a mountain of religious programming, afraid to exit the broom closet?

I recognized his mom as my mirror, showing me all the beliefs about witches I still harbored deep in the cobwebs of my mind.

Her automatic, unquestioned assumptions had made her instantly access the part of her brain where the word "witch" lived, and the only association she could conjure was horror. Included in her string of unquestioned assumptions was the conclusion that I should be insulted. *But was I?*

Baffled, yes. Dazed, yes. Insulted, no. Because of dangerous assumptions, she instantly chastised her son as if he had bitten someone. Her swift and emotionally charged reaction would have been more appropriate to her son calling me an expletive. He hadn't. He had called me a witch.

Mom could not have understood the gift her son handed me that day. The Divine had arranged a fortuitous meeting so a pint-sized messenger could deliver an important, in-your-face message to me: Stop hiding. Be who you are. What are you afraid of? Who are you afraid of?

You can see why I was shaken as I sat in my car, trying to process this. It wasn't just his words or where they landed on my inner terrain. It was because of how pierced-through I felt, how exposed, how utterly naked. All this from a six-year-old wielding three words. The universe is efficient.

Now that I'd been publicly outed by a little boy in a school parking lot— and had been permanently changed in an instant because of it—I had to ask myself those hard questions:

What *was* I afraid of?

What was I to do with the fearful and judgmental parts of my mind that were actively and purposely putting up resistance to my true nature, in the form of my husband and other people whose opinions I overvalued?

How had I allowed my husband's opinion to supersede my soul's calling to Tarot?

What was driving me to invest this much energy in self-denial?

If I did come out as a witch, effectively blowing my own cover, my whole world would turn on a dime. Was I ready for that?

The fact that you're holding this book in your hands and reading this story reveals the conclusions I found. I had to come out.

In the unfolding of my soul, I discovered what I had been afraid of: my own power.

I had no idea what would happen if I unleashed the magick that was coursing through my blood and stirring in my bones. This was an ancient, dark power. If I let myself say yes to it, would it gobble my soul?

What if I opened that door and didn't like what was on the other side? Would I be able to shut it again?

I was heading fast into uncharted territory, aided and abetted by a six-year-old child.

What I learned from that day, after many years of reflection, is that the universe will not idly stand by while I deny my self, my power, and my inner witch. Cosmic forces are ever turning in an infinite revelation of truth. None of us can escape who we are.

It's best to do the work of ruthless self-examination before we're forced to.

I no longer had to choose between owning up to being a witch or not. My only choice now was the timing. Would I do it now, as a proactive volunteer? Or would the universe have to continue to arrange fortuitous meetings and strange events to move me along on the true path of authenticity?

My close friend, a master teacher and healer, has a saying: "You can't do it wrong, but you can do it long."

I had been doing it long by being reactive. Fear was driving my vehicle.

Only I could decide the timeline for what I knew I had to do: bust out of the dusty broom closet and openly let the people in my life who love me know the truth: I am a witch.

I could either go willingly, joyfully, and happily as a surrendered soul to the greater purpose and calling of being a witch—or I could continue to resist, doubt, deny, and hurt myself.

Either way, the witch would not go away. Denying her as the deepest aspect of myself did not help me.

And why was I putting up all this fearful resistance? Because I was too afraid of living a deliciously and delightfully powerful and free life as a full-fledged witch? Because I was too afraid to wield powerful magick that rocks the world and upsets the status quo? Because I was too afraid to be exactly who I am—even though I know, deep within, that's all I really want to be?

This is lunacy, I thought to myself as I sat in the parking lot. *I have to make a choice, and I have to do it right now.* I had no other self-loving choice than to stand up for myself and who I knew myself to be.

I came out as a witch. Yes, it cost me relationships. Yet relationships that do not weather authenticity are not authentic relationships. I'm now surrounded by a circle of magickal practitioners who honor me as a powerful witch.

Thank you, wise six-year-old child. I don't remember your name, yet you are still with me.

Valerie Love

THE HEDGE WITCH AND THE SHAMAN

*T*he shaman called. He was troubled because his favorite, youngest son, the heir to his clan, was ill. The young boy was not responding to any of the medicines of his father, a long-trained elder who walked with strong energies.

The voice of Iron Walks with Two Fists was trembling, and he was as close to pleading as a man of his stature would allow when speaking to a woman.

"Come… do what you can. This is urgent. You say you have ability. This is a test I pray you pass."

I gathered my pouches and drove to the compound, where I found a dark pall. The clan members were sitting in a circle, silent, shaking rattles. The shaman gestured to the door, opened it, and said, "Do your work." Then he left.

The young boy was lying still, barely breathing. I wondered why his father didn't take him to the hospital, but I understood he held little faith in modern ways of healing.

The pressure to perform was enormous. I had to collect myself to shift from fear into my empty, clear-hearted healer's mind to assess the energy before me.

I set out my pouches, lit a candle, took a few deep breaths, and began. I lifted the boy's cold, pale leg and began "reading" some of the seventy-two pulses I am trained to interpret, to find out what was moving in his blood.

Having the information I needed, I began working with the many "voices of unseen ones." I took out my mortar and pestle and then opened the door and asked to see the spices in the kitchen. I found what was useful in the cupboards and set a pot of water to boil.

I asked a member of the rattling group to go fetch river mud and some plants that grew near the edge of the field. I started grinding the herbal elders I had in my pouches and poured them into the boiling water, to prepare a tea. Mixing spices from the kitchen rack with the found mud and plants, I prepared a poultice.

I undressed the weak child and smeared the earthy poultice over various organs and the bottoms of his feet. Then I wrapped him up in his blanket, tight as a burrito, hoping he would soon sweat. I dropped tiny drops of the tea over his cracked, dried lips for about an hour.

I sang healing songs.

After another hour, his breathing began to deepen. He began to cough and spit out thick, grey globs of phlegm. I called for a helper to sit with him while I returned to the kitchen to cut up roots and twigs for a broth. I added some chicken bones.

When I returned with the steaming mixture, the boy was sitting upright in bed and had a bit of color in his face. I smiled at him and said, "You are here now! Sip this soup slowly while it's hot." He picked up the spoon and, while I held the bowl, he ate.

Within the hour, he began looking more alive. I took the bowl from his hands, grateful and deeply relieved.

Once more, I monitored his pulses and found them to be gaining clarity, strength, and life force. I gave thanks and sang songs to the unseen ones, to the medicine keepers, and to the lineage teachers who had trained me. They had helped me restore the boy to health and return him to his clan.

Feeling only gratitude and relief, I rolled up my sheets, put my tools away, and cleared my pouches. Then I bowed my head, and leaving the child with the clan, said my goodbyes and walked out of the compound.

I heard the rattles shift their beat as I entered my car.

I had passed the test.

KJ Wolf

THE WEAVER OF TIME

t was a beautiful and hot summer day as I strolled along the main square of Lagos in Portugal. Suddenly, I realized I was standing on the Zocalo, where slavery began several hundred years ago. In front of me, I saw the Museum of Slavery. Next to it was a small, round building that belongs to the military. There was an exhibition.

I entered the windowless building and, guided by my intuition, walked to the back of the small, circular hall. I found a huge portal door decorated with yellow brown glass. Despite the beautiful work of the artists, I felt sad. A heaviness descended on me that made it hard to breathe.

An old woman, whose wrinkles ran through her face like furrows of time, stared at me, expressionless. Her presence seemed cold and forbidding, as if she wanted to chase me out of the building with her gaze. However, I stood still and breathed deeply in and out, trying to concentrate.

This building was full of history, but unfortunately, the story was a sad one. I could feel that slaves were kept here. Some were sold and others died. The Portuguese city of Lagos had been a port of call for slave ships from Africa in the 15th century. From here, captured people were further distributed into

Portugal and Europe. Most of them, robbed of their freedom and everything they owned, came from Africa.

In a moment, when the staring lady left the room, I felt a nearby spirit, a soul that was trapped on earth.

When he came closer, I could see him clearly. He wore a pair of tattered red pants, or what was left of them. Metal chains hung from his hands and legs. He appeared to be in his early twenties. The attitude on his round face was that of a warrior, yet engraved in him was the incomprehensible, horrible story of the slaves. His eyes were full of pain. He never spoke to me, but we communicated mentally.

When he asked me for help, I was surprised. I could feel my heart beating faster and I swallowed tears of sadness. My being was flooded with compassion as I felt this spirit's strength, beauty, and need. My respect was mixed with fear. *What spirit was I calling? And what powers would be awakened if I helped him?*

Finally, compassion won over doubt. I promised him that I would come back…

I was born in Bremen in 1974. My life was normal until my father died of lung cancer when I was seven. His death was so sudden, I didn't really have time to say goodbye.

I can still remember that, at that time, I didn't really understand what it meant to die. I often waited at the door for him to come back from work with his briefcase. But he never came back.

Instead, he showed up in my dreams, where he talked to me. Even though he wasn't physically there, I felt him near me as if he was still present. No one told me that I was communicating with a spirit. At that time, nobody from my family could explain this to me. I had to learn this years later, when I began following a spiritual path to understand myself better.

Two days after I left the Zocalo, I felt a call to return to the slavery museum. I looked all over Lagos for a flower store, but somehow, everything was closed that day. As I passed a cafe on my way back to the sea, I ran into Faith, a German acquaintance. We drank coffee and chatted about the community where we had met, where we had both slept in tents. Then I told her that I planned to perform a ceremony.

Suddenly the outside world faded around me and I felt the African spirit again. His presence was so strong this time that tears ran down my cheeks.

"Something unusual is happening here," Faith said, looking at me strangely. "I can sense something around us."

I quickly described my museum experience and added, "That's why I want to do a ceremony."

Without hesitation, Faith said, "I'd like to help."

We headed to the Zocalo—the main square—collecting wildflowers as we went. From the moment we entered the square, it seemed as if linear time stood still. We approached an African woman with a black dog roaming around the slave museum. She pointed at the museum and stammered, "Nothing is good. So much suffering. How…can I…" She began to cry.

The woman was hungry and homeless, so we bought her some food and talked for a while until we felt it was time to move on. As soon as we entered the building, I saw that the area where I wanted to do the ceremony was closed. Two elderly Frenchmen sat at the door as guardians.

"Can you unlock this for us?" I asked one of them.

He seemed to guess what we were about to do. With a mysterious smile, he replied, "You bring good energies so that this place can be purified, isn't it so?" And then he winked.

Despite his benevolent manner, he unfortunately did not have a key for the door, so we said goodbye. He dismissed us with the words: "Tonight there was a seaquake. It had a 4.2 magnitude. Not one of the biggest ones, but I felt some subtle shaking. It was a message. Anyway, have a good ceremony!" Then, with a huge grin, he turned and pulled his surly colleague back into the darkness of the building.

There we stood, surrounded by tourists, waiting under the scorching summer sun. The heavy sadness of the past was undeniable—but what could I do?

We placed a pink lily on the dark wooden door to call in beauty, and then turned around and gathered our courage. We approached the gate, each of us standing on one side, and I began to breathe my prayers of liberation into the flower.

The High Andes shamans, my teachers, had taught me that sometimes it is important to fill a place with light energy, to uplift it. I rattled, whistled, and called my spiritual guides. I requested that, on an energetic level, the door would open so that all the spirits who were still "trapped" there would move into the light.

A huge channel of pure light built up and began streaming to us from the upper world. The light flushed away the vast sadness, loneliness, bewilderment, and pain of this place and these spirits, into the depths of Mother Earth so that the energy could be transformed. I trembled, tears streaming down my face.

Suddenly, on the energetic level, the wing doors opened, and I could see into the interior of the building outside of time. There stood about a hundred slaves, all staring into the opening in disbelief. It was as if their souls had to remember what freedom was.

I encountered a heavy energy and surrendered to the Great Spirit in trust. I kept praying, singing, and whistling. My rattle flew, catching the burdensome energies.

The African spirit I had seen on my first visit was the first to step out of that fabricated prison and into the open air. Everyone else, at least a hundred of them, followed his lead. They stood in the pure light as their souls were cleansed by spirit. I both saw and sensed them.

My understanding of this situation was growing. I had not experienced the massive injustice of slavery during this lifetime, but I had learned how sadness and fear can eat at your soul. I knew that the temptation of revenge can strike anyone who is oppressed. Sometimes we cannot fully forgive those who have committed these great wrongs. Sometimes giving ourselves self-compassion is the biggest quantum leap we can manage.

Within myself, I bowed to these spirits and whispered, "May all spirits and people live in freedom."

Suddenly, the air seemed to flicker and shimmer. The fragrance of sweet flowers blew in with the wind and in an instant, the spirits vanished.

Faith and I looked at each other, smiling and relieved. The spirits were free. What had felt so heavy was now harmonious, and peace found its way into our hearts. We thanked all forces, closed the portals, and went to the sea. Yet somehow, I knew that this was not over.

As we approached the harbor entrance, I felt a sense of liberation. While I gratefully gazed at the open horizon and could glimpse Casablanca in the distance, Faith danced on the pier opposite Fort Ponta da Bandeira. Her footsteps said, *Fly, fly back to the shores of what you call home...*

That night, a whirling wind woke me up. I was lying in my tent, close to Lagos. Huge eucalyptus trees surrounded the place. While I was in between the dreaming and the waking world, I heard the dogs barking and the wind roaring. This wind was a primordial power that did not touch the ground, whirling over the treetops instead. The scenery was more than otherworldly. And something was about to happen...I felt it.

Then, in an instant, I sensed the African spirit standing in front of my tent, observing me. My body felt cemented to my bed. I could not move. Behind him stood hundreds of other spirits. Their power was so tremendous that, for a moment, my breath caught.

I sent him a thought: *What are you doing here?*

He smiled and said, *We will protect you whenever you call us. We are grateful for what you did.*

Then they disappeared, entering the moving energy vortex of the whirlwind. They were taken out of this world and up, toward the source, back to the light.

I forced myself to stand up and walk out of my tent. I looked up into the starry night where the silhouettes of the eucalyptus trees hovered like giants, doing their last work as messengers of the Divine. Now I sensed that the work was finally done. The spirits had left this plane.

In the darkness of the night, I remembered the meaning of the eucalyptus trees. By revealing ourselves and awakening our core truths and fears, we can act with confidence. This inner "reckoning" helps us become a person of integrity and truth as we move through obstacles we had considered insurmountable.

I felt a deep connection to these spirits. I realized now that I had lost my innocence, my primal trust, when I lost my father. My child's soul mourned him and longed for his return. Now I understand that nothing is separate from each other. On another level, my father is still there for me.

I was so grateful that I could help these souls in their transition to return to a place of peace, so that the thread of their ancestry might be healed again and woven into hope and harmony.

The weaver of time had brought us together to guide my understanding that everything is related, and that time is not linear. Everything is happening in one moment of time: the eternal now.

Annette Assmy

TALKING OUT THE FIRE

I lay on my stomach, at the hearth's edge, staring into the flames of the open fire as it danced and leapt about. The smell of burning wood and the familiar crackling and snapping of the fire lulled me into a dreamy state as I listened to my mother regale me with stories of my maternal ancestors. I soon found myself drifting far away as I imagined those special women who had lived so long ago.

Keziah Rose was my maternal great-great grandmother. My family was immensely proud of her. She was a full-blooded Cherokee Indian whose father was one of the most feared warriors of the tribe. But Keziah was born long after her father's warring days and grew up as an anglicized citizen in the Blue Ridge Mountains of North Carolina. She was well-known in her small community as a "fire talker," a person who had the ability to talk the fire from burns. Keziah was also the community's midwife, root-doctor, and faith healer, and was routinely called upon for her unique healing abilities. She regularly utilized an arsenal of medicinal plants such as the leaves from the Gilead tree—a poplar and cottonwood hybrid—plus bloodroot, goldenseal, ginseng, mullein, and black cohosh. Keziah passed down her knowledge of the healing arts to her daughter Rebecca. In turn, Rebecca instructed her daughters, Carrie Lee and Letitia, in the art of healing.

The coveted teachings continued to flow down through my maternal bloodline to my mother and were bestowed upon me when I was a child of five years. In addition to healing, my mother was an intuitive who "knew" things that had happened or were about to happen. She sometimes received this information through dreams and at other times spontaneously. She was a psychic who regularly relied on her sixth sense to interpret the world around her.

Knowing I had inherited these abilities, my mother impressed their sacredness upon me. I knew these abilities had been present in the maternal bloodline for centuries but could easily be taken away if misused. She taught me to practice in reverence and to never use my gifts for material gain.

I was taught how to "talk out the fire" through the proper hand movements, using my breath as an energy enhancement while silently saying, "There came a wolf from the east and an owl from the west bringing fire and frost. In frost, out fire—in the name of Yo Ho Wah." The phrase, Cherokee in origin, was to be repeated three times and never said aloud, only silently.

I was subsequently taught the secrets of the forests and how to use their abundant bounty to create potions, herbal salves, and poultices. By the time I was seven years old, my healing abilities had become well-known in the neighborhood. I soon found myself "laying hands" on my friends' sick or injured animals.

One afternoon during the Thanksgiving holiday, my father came to tell me my cat, Tom, had been hit by a car. I was devastated to see my beloved kitty lying unresponsive in a cardboard box on the back porch. His hindquarters had been severely injured. We were too poor to afford the care of a vet, so he was expected to die from his injuries. But I swore at that very moment that I would not allow him to die. Healing Tom became my mission. I spent every waking moment with him, "laying on hands," whispering comforting words, and willing him to live. I had fed and cared for him all day, every day, until he began to show signs of recovery. At first, he could only drag himself about—but over time, he began to stand for short periods, and then finally walk. Tom recovered fully and lived several more years. None of my family was surprised by Tom's recovery, and neither was I.

The 1970s rolled around and I became a student of astrology, numerology, Tarot, I Ching, palm reading, and esoteric religions. During high school, I gained the reputation of being a witch. Perhaps this was due to the way I dressed, typically in black and adorned with jewelry consisting of silver crosses and red roses. Maybe it was because I practiced palm reading and numerology between classes. Some students were afraid to come near me, but the majority, especially the females, sought me out for readings. I reveled in this practice and continued to treat my fellow students upon request.

When I was sixteen, I underwent a tonsillectomy and had an OBE—an out-of-body experience. Upon recovery, I realized I had developed the ability to see the human energy field, more commonly known as the human aura. My healing abilities were immediately enhanced because I could now see the exact layer of energy in which to "lay on hands." This catapulted me into a higher level of healing and I subsequently explored methodologies beyond what I had learned as a child.

Over the next decade, I attended retreats and conferences—any venue that offered me additional opportunities to develop my unique gifts. I learned and practiced meditation, yoga, and mindfulness. In my early thirties, I had a near-death experience. Again, my energy was transformed; when I recovered, I could see energy coming not only from humans, but from plants and animals. I felt changed physiologically, too. I was unable to switch on a light without blowing the bulb. I could not grocery shop because I was constantly shocked with arcs of blue light whenever I touched the shelving. I found that streetlights would go out as I walked past them.

Fortunately, I had recently begun my professional career at a leading medical university and hospital where complementary and alternative medicine (CAM) was routinely practiced. I developed a strong relationship with a CAM physician and a physics professor. Both women recognized my unique healing gifts. They conducted several experiments in the physics lab using Kirlian photography to measure the coronal discharges of energy coming from my hands. The experiments, which involved an intervention and a control group, yielded data that supported healing at a molecular level.

Following these experiments, I enrolled in a healing touch curriculum at the medical university. The hospital offered this methodology as an in-patient service. I gained a level four practitioner certification and subsequently worked on numerous hospital patients, as well as a number of family and friends.

In the years following, I sought additional training and certification in shamanic drumming and healing; past-life regression; and spiritual dowsing. By practicing these modalities, I further enhanced my natural abilities and supercharged my chakras, especially the third eye chakra.

As a student of history and anthropology, I have long recognized that, had I been born in another time, I might have been labeled a "witch," ostracized from society, and perhaps put to death for my abilities and belief systems.

I use my witch abilities every day. I use the power of my hands to heal and energize my cats, my husband, my friends and family, wild birds, and injured animals. I routinely conduct energy work in my vegetable and flower gardens. I talk to the plants, trees, and rocks in my yard, thanking them for their beauty. I collect feathers that seem to drop out of nowhere and use them during my healing and cleansing rituals. My connection to nature is strong and my roots go deep into Mother Earth's consciousness.

I embrace the witch in me because I know it is my true self and my true calling, passed down to me through the ages. I live my life in gratitude to the women who came before me, for their strength and fearlessness in practicing their art and their tireless service to those in need.

Pamela D. Nance

AMATERASU AND THE MOON RABBIT

I had been seeking more…

While shamanic journeying—etheric questing, as I like to call it—on a few occasions, I have come across a white rabbit. Once, on a full moon, the rabbit made me a moon elixir. At that time, I had thought it was enough. And it was… at the time.

As a child, one of my favorite stories was the Chinese tale about a woman and her rabbit ascending to the sky. With my naked eye, I could see the body of a rabbit in profile on the surface of a bright, full moon. I would search for the outline as often as I could, and I do this even now. The view and what I recalled hearing of the story fascinated me as a child. Throughout my life, I would call the outline profile the Moon Rabbit and I have a vague memory of it being called Rabbit on the Moon.

I was not as interested in the woman in the story, whose arms held the rabbit in the sky. In hindsight, I should have paid more attention to her, to better understand what I was seeking.

It had been so long since I had heard the story—at least three decades. Throughout my life, I'd heard references to *self* being tied to the moon and its cycles. I knew that during full moons, emotions are high and things out of the ordinary occur. I was always super careful with myself during these times. I tried not to fall into a "label," as my work is challenging enough without the extra stigma.

A few months later, while on another quest searching for more, I came across the Japanese sun goddess, Amaterasu. Since I do not have clairaudient powers, I try to talk to beings and then just observe their answers based on what they are emoting. Each time I came across Amaterasu, she was gazing at some kind of screen, but I could not see clearly what it was. And I could never see her face, only her back. However, looking from her vantage point—either behind her or beside her—everything was always luminescent and golden.

One day, I had asked Amaterasu to show me what she was trying to convey. Our journey took us to a small village near a lake. As she pulled a sun disk from her pocket, I saw the Moon Rabbit running toward the lake from another direction. It stopped at the lake and it looked like it was making an elixir. Although I could not see clearly, since arriving at the lake, more beings had arrived and were gathering. I could just feel the anticipation, the murmuring of the crowd.

By this time, Amaterasu raised herself in the sky and held the sun disk just so, and then the Moon Rabbit poured the elixir into the lake and the lake suddenly became a portal. Slowly, selected individuals present made their wishes into the portal and the beings or the items appeared. When it was my turn to receive what was for me, a huge being emerged from the portal and started chasing me!

I began to think, *Is this really supposed to happen? Should I leave the meditation now? What exactly did I wish for? What am I supposed to be learning at this moment?* Because really, it is hard to think when something is chasing you!

Luckily, one of the members of the crowd had a gift of taming. And as they activated their gift, the being that was chasing me stopped. By now, Amaterasu had closed the portal and the Moon Rabbit had jumped into her arms. I then looked over to the creature that had been chasing me, now as docile as a lamb. I realized that this being wanted to become part of my spirit team to help bring me into balance. It was a gift from Amaterasu, the Moon Rabbit, and the being that tamed this newest addition.

And now, I know what I was seeking was not *more*. I had been seeking balance.

Dawn M. Kubo

ANUBIS AND THE WITCH

"*H*e thinks you're a witch, Donna!" my teacher said. The thought pushed up against all my senses as I replayed those words in my head again and again. The teacher cackled.

I felt confused and thrown off-kilter. I never ever thought of myself with that designation before. *What's a witch anyway?* I mused. *Am I a witch?*

Her brash statement, served up with a sneer, threw me back energetically. *Is she insulting me?* It sure felt like it. I tend to think of myself as a star girl, and she knows it. I am one born of light, from the heavens. I know in every cell of my being that I am from far, far away. Here for a while, and not for much longer.

Witches are from this place called Earth, and I am not from this Earth! I exclaimed in my internal dialogue.

A few hours prior to this engagement, I had pretended to be a tourist while meandering through the shrine of Anubis at the Mortuary Temple of Queen Hatshepsut in Egypt. Wearing a crisp, white, button-down shirt and smart-looking, royal blue camping pants, I located my target. The trendy white sneakers accented with gold stripes that I had slipped on that morning were a modern-day spin on the magickal, golden-winged shoes of the Greek god Hermes. His brilliant golden shoes enabled him to fly through unseen realms and conduct psychopomp. This skill, otherwise known as "soul conduction," is something I've been graced with and since I had my golden shoes on, I knew I'd be traversing the etheric planes on this day.

As my feet locked into the location I was destined for, I noticed that I was just steps away from an impressive painting of Anubis in all his glory. The artist had captured the jackal-headed god's essence just marvelously. There Anubis sat, erect, with a golden kilt wrapped around his waist. He flaunted a pale blue, fitted top that hugged his broad chest and shoulders. He radiated regality, confidence, and high purpose. It was hard to look away as he captivated me with his stateliness and vibrancy.

I should adopt that posture! He is so poised, I thought to myself.

Then I remembered a law of nature from my yoga studies back in the states. It had to do with alignment and how one could master advanced yoga poses simply by aligning the body optimally. In that moment, I realized this tenet was profound! The words I remembered were, "If you line it up, you'll open it up." And I realized the "it" was not just the physical body but the light body channel connection to Source or God or All That Is. With that, I stood up taller, drew my shoulders back, and lifted my chin slightly so it was level with the earth.

And then, I remembered.

I had anchored into this location because it held something for me: a memory and a mission. It was here that my connection with Anubis became more pronounced in my consciousness. I recalled that I'd been here before, in other lifetimes. This ancient god and I had been acquainted through the ages, and apparently still are. I knew he was the ferryman—in other words, he crossed souls over into other realms, just like I did (and my other friend, Hermes). In that moment of revelation, the corners of my mouth turned upwards and created a soft smile upon my face.

I turned to gaze again upon the exquisite wall mural and noticed that the temple guard was watching me. He seemed to know what I was thinking, and he snickered. It came to me that we were old friends, too, and I suspect it came through to him as well, because in the blink of an eye, we both burst out laughing as though someone had told us the funniest of jokes. We were completely in sync, even though neither one of us spoke the other's language and we'd never been introduced. This was a true soul connection.

Without delay, I felt compelled to work. I moved my hands briskly and created intricate designs that punctured the quantum field as I simultaneously spoke in an ancient language. This wasn't new to me; I'd been consciously engaging with higher aspects of myself like this for years. I'd spoken hundreds of languages, otherwise known as "light language." My hands and fingers moved as fast as hummingbird wings beat. I am not only fast, but I am also precise with the symbols I create. These symbols are a form of sign language that can be used as a communication bridge linking planes of existence.

Sometimes I do get over excited and really go to town. And this was one of those days. I was in Egypt with a soul brother to my left watching my back as I anchored into the depths of remembrance. *What could go wrong?* I thought. And then, something did…

Typically, I cloak myself and hide in plain sight. But here I was with a friend, an old buddy, and in a place I remembered from so long ago that it felt like home. I felt safe. On my right side, however, was a foe. I hadn't noticed him there before, because I was so enthralled with the intensity of this place and with my old acquaintances. Only yards away on my right, this clean-cut man wearing a sports shirt buttoned up to his neck had been watching the scene, unbeknownst to me. This man, with outrage painted upon his face, began screaming at the guard, my old friend, and pointing at me in horror.

At first, I was confused. Everything had been going so well! I was connecting to this ancient place and to my memories of being here lifetimes ago, and suddenly this man had ripped me out of my trance state and back into the 108-degree day my body was sweating in. It felt like an assault—and, it was! I had been in my own space, minding my own business, and he began screaming at me. I wasn't even speaking aloud, just quietly, under my breath.

Once I regained myself and realized what had occurred, I began to laugh. Big, deep belly laughs. Then I looked at my friend and he began to laugh, too.

How dare this man throw a fit and attempt to ostracize me in my temple, this temple of Anubis that my soul remembered so dearly, I thought to myself.

Clearly, he had no idea how far back in time the guard and I went. We were old chums. I had also been friends with the great being I saw painted on the wall before us, who almost came to life through the deeply saturated paint that created his form.

When this man was unsuccessful at silencing me and binding my hummingbird hands, which whirred louder than my voice through the veil, he stomped off. I figured I'd better boogie on out of there before he came back with someone without a sense of humor, who might scold me, or worse, for being who I am. As I bid farewell, the guard motioned for me to hand him my camera so he could take a quick picture. And in a snap, I had a nice little memento of our time together that I will never forget.

I exited this hall of Anubis and descended a massive staircase in the middle of a golden desert that I recalled walking along solemnly in procession, long ago. This time, however, I had a bounce in my step. My mission was accomplished. I had inner fulfillment in my heart and the memory that I needed to fit into the puzzle I'd been putting back together—the puzzle called me.

Later that day, my teacher's flippant comment nagged at me like a splinter that you just can't extract—something you cannot see but can feel sharply. This unrelenting irritation sent me on a walk down memory lane and I began to reminisce about my potential witchy nature. My slender wooden wand, lovingly hand wrapped with copper wire and sporting a pink pearl affixed to the tip, came to mind instantly. I acquired her in Sedona, Arizona at a rock shop that, come to think of it, a witch owned. This wand is delicate yet powerful, like me. She has laser-like precision swathed in sweetness and can mitigate the pain of deep healing work with the slightest touch—which, I realized, is also like me.

It then occurred to me how much attention I place upon sourcing and empowering the sacred oils and herbs I use to heal myself and others. It's innate to attune to the wisdom of the plant and I just know what to use and how much to use for a particular remedy. The spirit of the plant talks to me and whispers this Divine knowledge into my ears.

I recalled how I harness the power of incantations; how I make magickal healing potions that elevate the atmosphere; how I clear homes of unwelcome energies and entities; and how I cross souls over to their destination in the afterlife. And how could I forget about my fascination with television shows about witches! I devour these shows and love the oldies and goodies from the 1960s, the witchy shows of modern times, and everything in between.

And just like that, I exclaimed, "Oh my goddess, I *am* a witch!"

It was suddenly so obvious that I am not only a witch, but a practicing witch!

How could I have denied this truth? I wondered. Memories swirled in my head and I felt dizzy and nauseous.

I, a witch, have demeaned myself. I've demeaned this aspect, demeaned the blessings I've been allotted in this lifetime. I know, in the core of my being, that I've earned my blessings from many other timelines in which I embodied sacred wisdom.

How could I have expected that man at the temple of Anubis to accept me and my ways when I hadn't yet fully embraced this aspect of myself? I'd welcomed back so many of my aspects, especially those that pertain to my galactic roots—but not this one. The sickness that overtook me explained a lot. The title of witch has so many negative connotations. Witches have been persecuted. Witches have been targeted. Witches have been vilified. It's no surprise I'd deny such an association.

Even though I take on the persona of bravery, fear lies buried deep within me. I sensed it was related to those wise women called witches who were extinguished.

Was I extinguished and thrown away like trash? I didn't wonder for long, because the answer that came was *Yes*. I knew in my heart that there would be much to rectify. But first, it was essential to claim my truth and honor this aspect of me. I needed to fit this piece with great care into the puzzle that is me.

And as I did, I affirmed, "I am a witch."

Donna Kuebler

THE HAIL STORM

had always dreamed of visiting Sedona, Arizona to enjoy its red rocks and healing aura. Enduring many surgeries had left me depleted and weak.

As I recovered, I happened to see something about the mystery school founded by Rev. Valerie Love. It was my invitation to live out a dream.

Walking around in Sedona, I had no idea the healing I would receive nor the changes the universe was sending my way. Hiking with the mystery school brought life back to my body, mind, and soul. It was a wonderful trip.

But when I returned home, my heart suddenly broke into pieces. My inner resistance began to manifest, all at once.

I had prearranged to fly back to Sedona that weekend. As I gripped my first, first-class ticket, I was in tears, knowing I had a choice to make. Should I cancel my plans and try to figure out what my resistance was all about? Or should I try to keep moving forward?

My daughter, who had heard me crying, said, "Mom, you are my example. If you don't follow your dreams, then how will I follow mine?"

Her words fueled me to call my mentor.

"Everything is messed up! I'm shattered!" I told her. "I feel broken. How can I move forward?"

Rev. Valerie replied, "I can't wait to see you again."

As we talked about my resistance, my decision became obvious. I would go back.

After making sure my family was steady, I managed to board the flight, but a storm raged inside me. I was flooded with emotions: hurt, betrayal, and pain. I doubted my choice to press forward.

When I feel this way, I usually avoid people. My ego tells me to hide. Then I become depressed as I watch myself fall apart. After a short time, I remember my purpose. This was a familiar cycle that I was ready to break.

Back in Sedona, hiking again with the mystery school, all I could feel was my tumultuous inner storm. But something magickal and unimaginable was about to happen.

When we arrived at Amitabha Stupa and Peace Park, I was initially thrilled to see the things and places I had dreamed about, despite the massive fear and sadness that clouded my joy. The worst emotional pain I've ever felt in my life gripped me. I did my best to not focus on it.

At the Amitabha Stupa and Peace Park medicine wheel, we were instructed to keep silent and go into prayer. I heard the words, *Go inside yourself. Prepare your mind before walking around this medicine wheel, so you can get what you need.*

The wheel had been recently used for ritualistic purposes by the Native Americans. Pink and white flowers were strewn everywhere. My hope was that, through prayer, I might tap into the spiritual realm and go to spirits who had already been summoned. Maybe my request wasn't too late. Maybe this had been prepared for me.

I began saying my prayer as I walked around the medicine wheel.

I called out to God and asked for help from the archangels of the four corners—Archangel Michael, Archangel Raphael, Archangel Uriel, and Archangel Gabriel. I needed the spirit realm to hear me.

As I moved forward, imagined obstacles came to stop me in my tracks. "I'm here, Archangels," I said. "Hear me. Native Spirits, hear me."

As I walked around the medicine wheel saying these words, I prayed, "Give me a sign. I need to get past my disbelief that I can't handle whatever is coming next."

I walked a few more steps and said, "Archangel of the West, hear me!"

A piece of ice struck me, and then another struck the ground ahead of me. I began to feel hail falling from the sky—in the desert, in the middle of a sunny day!

I was walking, and God was meeting me. As I prayed, the hail increased and the winds blustered mightily. A cloud began to encroach on the sun as the storm within me manifested all around me.

Upon completing my walk of the medicine wheel, I received my sign. The storm stopped and the full sunshine returned.

My heart became free.

Icy Kendrick

FROM PENTECOSTAL TO PRACTICING MAGICK

*a*s I was growing up, whenever I had moments of great doubt—when I was feeling like I didn't know who I was, or what I was—my grandmother, Eula, steered me toward scripture. She told me to repeat Psalm 139:14, King James version: "I will praise thee; for I am fearfully and wonderfully made: marvelous are thy works; and that my soul knoweth right well."

The Pentecostal Church was our livelihood, our haven, and our arena of God and the Holy Ghost. Unfortunately, that was not how I felt for most of my childhood. People around me never told me about spirituality, or any path to the Divine, other than being a Pentecostal.

But it was also a sacred practice that pounded pulpits about eternal damnation for anyone who was a different sexuality, spirituality, or ilk. It was a place of vividly expressed religious extremism that included speaking in tongues, casting out demons, anointing the sick, prophesying, shouting, and running the aisles, and using music to shake up the energy of the congregation.

Many skeptics and outsiders see this type of religion as bizarre and shocking. But to those of us who were practitioners, it was home. The church was the place where I first started to feel energies and vibrations rising up through my core, and the first place where I started seeing spirits—in the church windows, around corners, and even in the pews during services. Outside the four walls of the church house, spirits and spirit activity started to appear more vividly in my daily life.

The first time I remember seeing a spirit outside of church was at my grandmother's farm. A beautiful, old-fashioned lady in white walked across the farmyard and into the garden one evening, right at dusk. I asked the elders of my family for advice. Why was I seeing this apparition? They reassured me that seeing spirits was one of the wiles of Satan.

But if that were true, why was I, as a devoted Pentecostal boy, seeing spirit activity? Why was I able to feel what the departed souls were doing and what they were feeling? How would someone explain that?

For the next several years, I saw many other spirits, and I started to realize that I was magic. I would have a vision or dream of an event happening, and it always had a way of becoming true. When I was seventeen, my mother and stepfather bought a small truck for me so that I could have more freedom and more responsibility. One night, after driving the truck for a few months, I had a vivid dream that I would wreck that truck and die a bloody and gruesome death. I awoke sweating and in a panic. I started to have that dream so often, I became terrified to drive that truck even a few miles from home.

At age eighteen, I got a job over the mountain in Chattanooga, Tennessee. I would travel almost daily over the winding curves and dangerous switchbacks of the hills. One afternoon, when driving home from work in a fierce rainstorm, I came around a curve … and the next thing I knew, I was regaining consciousness, sitting on the passenger side door of the truck. My truck rested on its side, having flipped over. The seatbelt pressed against my neck, and the area around me was spattered with shards of broken glass and splashes of blood.

I remember an elderly man beating on the windshield glass and then helping me climb up on the steering wheel and out the driver's side door. As I sank down to the asphalt of the wet highway, the man asked me, "Are you okay, son?" I nodded but rested my head between my knees.

People in a nearby house had heard the noise and rushed to help me. I kept asking them, "Where is he? Where's that man?"

They told me there had been no man helping me. They denied seeing him. But I know that I saw him, clear as day. I genuinely believe the gentleman was an angel or guardian spirit.

The next few years, as I grew in my spirituality, I began to have conversations and encounters with the supernatural on a regular basis. This was when I became curious about witchcraft and the occult. Growing up Pentecostal, I had seen so much of that religion. Now I noticed, as I began studying magick and witchcraft, that many of the messages and practices of the Pentecostal Church aligned with witchcraft.

It wasn't long before I realized that I was a witch—and not just any witch. I was a Christian Folk Witch. I fiercely believed in God, Jesus, and the Holy Ghost—but I couldn't deny my natural calling and natural desire for magick and mysticism. I started referring to God as the Universe and the Divine.

In the words of the prophet Jeremiah, "It's like a fire shut up in my bones."

I couldn't stop growing in my craft as I became more aware of my truth and my genuine self. Crystals called out to me. I started learning how to use assorted types of roots and herbs, and I learned more about spirits and angels. The saints of Catholicism became the muses and companions that I worked with and petitioned. I was infatuated and amazed at the knowledge I was absorbing.

Still, in the back of my mind, a ghost from my past lingered: God.

Learning about magic, witchcraft, and the occult was my passion and my sole focus in life. But I couldn't shake the feeling that I was somehow *wrong*—and that if the trumpet of Archangel Gabriel should sound, I would be left behind to burn for all eternity in the pits of hell with all the other sinners. I began having wild dreams about demons tearing at my heels as I dashed along stone paths crossing lakes of fire. I saw the souls of the tormented being destroyed for their sins.

I fell into a dark depression and felt hopeless, alone, and confused.

Was I supposed to abandon my true calling as a witch—or was I to rejoin the Pentecostal Church that I felt had condemned me? I couldn't leave behind my knowledge of witchcraft, but now I was terrified of eternal damnation. I thought about suicide every moment of the day, and I attempted twice to end my life. Somehow, in all the pain, I mustered the courage to rejoin the church. I became a member, got baptized in the Holy Ghost and fire again, and became a warrior for God.

It was hard, but I destroyed and did away with every aspect of my life that was witch-inspired. I pushed aside my natural calling and refused to acknowledge the spirit world around me. My new passion was spreading the Gospel of Jesus Christ. I became deeply involved in the church and "winning souls" for Christ. I thought I was doing what I was called to do.

But a still, small voice deep inside me called me to something else. Witchcraft and magick kept pulling me back on the pathway to the Divine. I felt the call repeatedly for the next year of my life. A constant battle between witch and Christian was playing out in my heart—between doing what the Bible said, and doing what came naturally. My old friend, depression, came knocking back on my heart's door once again, along with the desire to end my life. I felt hopeless and abandoned. What would I do? Turn to God, or be my true Divine self? Life kept forcing me to make a choice. Then one day, after months of being tormented not knowing what to do with my eternal soul, I realized something profound.

God *was* witchcraft, and witchcraft *was* God.

As if a lightbulb suddenly went off, truth interrupted the darkness that I had been wandering in for so long. It was just a small match head of light, but it illuminated my darkest thoughts and fears. I realized that God was *in* witchcraft, in every aspect of it. God, the Universe, and the Divine were all the same entity and the same energy.

Energy connects all things, creates and destroys all things, and *is* all things. The Pentecostal Church had taught that God was in everything. Now I understood that God is energy. Jesus is energy. The Holy Ghost is energy. I lost my fear of eternal damnation, because to me that had been a manmade concept anyway. I began to see that the Bible was a metaphor, not a literal basis for guiding human existence. I could love God, the Universe, and the Divine—and I could also be who I was born to be. The planets wouldn't fall from the heavens and the oceans wouldn't go dry. I was meant to be a witch, and by damned, I was going to be.

The veil of darkness over my life lifted then. It was a new day for me. I started integrating my craft and the church as one practice, and it worked for me! I started meditating again, and using crystals, and rosaries, and the Bible. The saints I had communed with were back in my life and flourishing with my craft, just like in olden times. Life was full of jubilee, and the world was back on its axis.

And then one day, the church caught on to my great awakening.

The Pentecostal leaders gave me only two options: I could throw out my new thinking or be excommunicated from the church. I struggled over the decision for the next few days, contemplating my final decision for my spiritual walk in this life. And then I made that decision which leads me to where I am today.

I am a practicing, powerful Christian Folk Witch. I was born a natural witch, and I will die as one. I commune with the saints and ask them to work on my behalf. I devote myself to working with the Blessed Mother, Mary, the mother of God. I also work with roots and herbs to bring change to my life and the lives of those around me.

I still experience spirit activity and communication with the departed. Candle work and divination are among my regular practices. I express myself and my feelings with herbal healing and being an empath. I make offerings to my ancestors and the spirits around me with libations, offerings, and altars. This is my passion.

My life and calling as a Christian Folk Witch is one of the biggest blessings that God has given me. To be my genuine self as a witch and to be aligned with the Divine, on this pathway to ascension, is the biggest honor in my life. Just as the Prophet Jeremiah said, "It's like a fire shut up in my bones."

Colton Berry

TINY WITCH

t is a few days before Christmas and the last day of school. When we depart today, we will be home for winter break. Two full weeks of absolutely no school, no getting up early, no braving winter's bone-chilling breath just to draw pictures and color; to learn letters, numbers, and words; and to hang out with newly made friends. The holiday would be about cartoons, overly sweet cereal in the mornings, and uninterrupted play all afternoon in the warm sanctuary of our rooms. This is extreme bliss to a post toddler.

The Christmas tree at the head of the class, next to the teacher's desk, is buried in a mountain of gifts that has been slowly growing as parents brought in their child's Pollyanna presents. Today is the day we will get to open them—and I have a front-row seat! I sit directly in front of the teacher because I'm the youngest child in the class and the shortest and she wants to keep her eyes on me.

I feel as if I'm being told, "Just pick the present you want, and it's yours." And somehow, I know this is true.

I have always been a witch, even before I exited the portal of my mother's womb and entered this realm. I descend from a lengthy line of powerful witches and magickal beings: healers, root workers, stitch witches, kitchen witches, and merfolk—both mermaids and mermen. How else could I possess the blazing fire that burns deep in my soul? This kind of power can only be wielded by a witch.

As a child, at the tender age of four, I knew I possessed the gift of energy manipulation. I did not know the scientific name for what I could do, but I knew I had the power to manifest things with thoughts. Of course, I did not call it *magic*. I just knew I could make things happen and influence others effortlessly.

And at that very moment, I spot the gift. It's beautiful. It calls to me from underneath the decorated paper, spiraling ribbons, and enormous bow. *Pick me... pick me ...* it commands in a hushed yet very assertive tone. It is the biggest gift in the pile, and I just know that it's mine.

This was where the magick began.

I felt a sense of urgency, so I went to work immediately, knowing speed was important. I had to ensure that this gift would go home with me. I set my intention and applied uninterrupted focus. I said the words aloud. It was simple, yet powerful and direct. Where was all this coming from? I did not know.

As I stared at the huge package intensely, I said what the voice in my head said: "You are mine! You will go home with me today!"

The hands of the huge, black-and-white clock that hung on the cinder block wall slowly inched around the diameter of the circle. Tick... tock... tick... tock ... the pace was maddeningly slow. I would occasionally glance at my gift with a smile, knowing the magick was already done and the spell was complete.

Once the Christmas party was in full swing, with its cake, cookies, candy, and laughter, I had all but forgotten the spell I cast earlier. We were having Kindergarten fun. Then the teacher said the precise words to snap me out of child's play.

"It's time to open your gifts!"

My attention shifted focus and I was no longer playing the role of a four-year-old child. I was a centuries-old witch ready to claim the fruits of my labor.

We all gathered in front of the tree as the teacher began calling out the names on the gift tags. Well, I already knew which one was mine, but I was impatient. It took so long! Was she waiting until the end to say the name on the biggest present?

Finally, the teacher called my name! "Last but not least...... come up and get your gift!"

Everyone stared at me as I confidently moved toward my gift. I felt short as I stood beside it, with its ribbons and enormous bow. Staring at the present when I cast the spell hadn't really given me an accurate perception of the magnitude of my gift.

I was so happy that my little fingers seemed not to be working. My teacher noticed and came to assist me. It was quite a job for the two of us to unwrap this gigantic toy. Somehow, we got the job done.

After the unveiling, I just stood there for what seemed like fifteen minutes... a long time for a kid. It was looking at *me*... This doll was the same color as me. She was my size and my height. She was *me!* I watched her with amazement, staring through the plastic, the only thing that separated our small faces. And a hint of satisfaction washed over me as I realized what I had done.

For I knew what had taken place, unbeknown to any of my classmates or my teacher. I had manifested the biggest gift next to the tree. I'd even made her look like me, so there would be no mistake about who was the rightful owner. The spell had worked much better than I thought. I took some time admiring my work.

I usually walked home from school, and I could not carry my new best friend home. She weighed just as much as me. So, my teacher had to call my parents to come pick me up.

Even as a child, I knew the importance of silence because the wisdom of the centuries old crone was very much alive inside my tiny body. I've never told this story to anyone until recently, and I am gracefully approaching fifty. I knew even then the secret code of the witch!

To Know

To Will

To Dare

To Keep Silent.

Queen Vashti

DISCOVERING THE WITCH WITHIN

efore I knew what a witch was, I knew that I wanted to be one. When I came to fully understand what a witch is, I realized that I already was one.

My journey to self-realization began in the late nineties in New York City. I was about twelve years old at the time. As a Catholic middle school student and the daughter of a devout Southern Christian, my life was about as far from magickal as a life could be. But all of that was about to change.

In 1998, a little television show called *Charmed* re-introduced me to the word "witch" and made me question everything I thought I knew about witches. It was a fictional show, but the impact it was about to have on my life was very real.

The show included everything a prime-time, late-nineties drama had to offer: attractive stars, celebrity cameos, and cheesy sci-fi special effects. But it wasn't those things that made me tune in week after week. It was *witchcraft* that captured my soul's attention. Every time the sisters would run up to the attic to consult their giant book of spells; or head to the kitchen to start throwing herbs and oils into a big pot of mystery potion; or sit in front of the city map with their pendulums poised to find this week's demon, my heart would race. I felt something unknown was calling me. There was something about this lifestyle that I wanted.

I embarked on a journey of seeking and learning about anything and everything "witch." My journey would take me to self-dedication as a Wiccan, a career as a Tarot reader, and a calling to practice reiki and energy healing. Throughout this time, I identified as a witch. But it would take nearly twenty-five years, and the hospitalization of my mother, before I fully understood what a witch is—and what I am.

Shortly before my thirty-sixth birthday, my mother was admitted to the intensive care unit after experiencing a minor stroke. I stayed with her for the week after her discharge from the hospital. To care for her physically, I made her nourishing fruit infusions and healing herbal baths. I gave her daily reiki sessions. To care for her spiritually, I made nightly offerings to the protective spirits of the land where her home is and I lit a white candle infused with prayer every morning for her speedy recovery. To keep order, I cooked and cleaned for her, maintained her garden, and played point person for all her doctor appointments. I fed her with recipes that she could continue to prepare for herself when I left.

These efforts paid off immensely. The energy in her home went from frightened and stressed to light and easy. Her health improved dramatically within days. I saw a noticeable excitement in her eyes over the herbal remedies that she was learning from me. In response to this, my mother began calling me various names to try to describe my service to her. She would say things like "Look at my daughter, what a wonderful nurse!" or "Thank you, professor, for all your help" or "Hold on, let me put you on the phone with my director." Depending on what I was doing for her at that moment, my title would change. After a while, I began to realize that the title kept changing because she couldn't quite settle on the right word to describe all that I could do.

What do you call someone who seems to flow with the universe rather than against it—who understands plants and medicine—who can change the energy of a space or situation with the pure power of their intention? At first, I couldn't put my finger on the right word for the role that I was serving for my mother.

On my last day there, it hit me like a ton of broomsticks. I came to the powerful realization that the word my mother was reaching for, but couldn't quite find, was "witch." When I realized this, tears began to well up in my eyes. For the first time in my magickal life, I fully understood what it meant to be a witch. And I finally understood why I was one. I understood that, without casting a spell or engaging in any type of formal witchcraft, I was witching every time I acknowledged and took control of the energy around me.

The term "witch" has meant different things to different groups of people throughout history. But for me, the witch is the wise one who knows their power and takes charge when needed. A witch knows how to heal, bring light into times of darkness, and empower others to do the same.

BronxWitch

A WITCH BY ANY OTHER NAME

I am magickal. The earth is my friend, my mother, and my angel. I still do not know her as well as I hope to. My life's journey includes a deeper acquaintance and a greater knowledge of that which sustains me. It is through the fruit of the earth's gifts, magickal and healing practices, and witchy wisdom that I deepen my acquaintance with myself.

In the world I grew up in, you'd never admit to being a witch. Heavens! That was considered pure evil. The idea of that world conjured nightmarish darkness and spells and all manner of wrongdoing. One didn't dare even say the word out loud!

Later I would understand that description was a distorted vision of a witch. Like most true things that empower, the negative depiction substituted, confused, and inverted truth to suit the purposes of an agenda that was life-denying and unnatural. Evil was just what a witch was not!

In my youngest days, I was aware of myself as part of Mother Nature, before I outgrew that "foolishness." As a girl, I had wandered through my backyard in search of answers to the mysteries of life. Moving about the garden, I sniffed each flower and tasted each berry. Nothing the grown folks told me made sense. I made spiders my friends and tried to keep them inside the house, in a jar with sticks and twigs. My seven-year-old mind determined that this habitat would be adequate for their needs. I felt devastated when, after several attempts to house them, the spiders would die—or disappear.

My sister and I did energy work, although I did not have a name for it then. I knew somehow that my hand gestures, moving about and over her chakras, were mystical and magickal. I waved my hands freely above her, knowing I was being guided to do what I did not consciously understand.

"Wait a minute, let me finish! There! Healed!" I pronounced at the end of my sessions. *How did I know that?*

I grew up "churched," so all the ancient, mysterious, "old-school" wisdom grew away from me. I got the impression that I needed to reject whatever stories and secrets Pachamama (Mother Earth) wanted to share with me. Her life was not as important as the day-to-day business of adjusting to the world of materiality and its directives. Go to school. Get an education. Check. Go to church. Be a good girl. Of course. Get a good job. Contribute and settle into status-quo living.

So I did all that, leaving my earthy explorations and interests behind. I abandoned my girlish ways. Life became dull. I endeavored to fit my round self into the square hole of routine living, and even though I felt totally out of place, I rolled along that way for years.

As time passed, various things piqued my interest. I was intrigued but not yet willing to think of myself as anything but an ordinary, normal woman tap dancing through life the best way that I could. Behind the scenes, however, I was reawakening and rediscovering my true self. *What was this meditation thingy that was all the rage? Yoga? Tai Chi? Crystals? Tarot cards? What do you mean they are "alive?"* I heard the voice of my religious training in my head saying, *Don't let them bind you with a spell!*

But… I wasn't making it as a regular person. Something continued to pull me further into my curiosity, back to the realms of my childhood magick and communion with the earth that sustains me. Nature gave me peace and strength. I took solace with the trees and nurturing from the rivers. I felt joy in wide-open spaces as I renewed my acquaintance with Mama Earth and her magic. I learned to appreciate the gifts of the earth as air, and herbs, and food, and water.

Alongside this rediscovery, I sought to know myself more deeply and in new and expanded ways. I began to pursue the study and practice of meditation. I explored spirituality through African traditional religions and through my Indigenous American heritage practices, through my spiritual heritage of Incan shamanism, and through Hinduism and Sufism. As this wisdom and so much more presented itself to me, I was brought into closer connection with the awareness of who I am.

I became acquainted with "spirits," and ancestral wisdom became a part of my experience and natural knowing. One night, I spoke with a witchy friend of mine who was incredulous that I had not seen those teddy bears where Mama bear has her big arms wrapped around her baby bear. That night, I suddenly awoke from my sleep when I realized that a spirit was embracing me in that very same way. A week or two later, I received a gift in the mail from my friend: a plush teddy bear Mama hugging her baby.

Time and new discoveries unfolded for me with a deeper understanding of the knowledge I had begun to acquire as a girl. I am a witch; I am a healer; I am a wise woman. I did not have those words for it back then, but my inner Divine always guided me and I acted accordingly. Now I know I am these things and so much more!

As I embraced life, I followed the things that felt correct and that brought me happiness and a sense of being supported, loved, and protected. Everything became clearer. I synced my conscious knowledge with my ever-expanding awareness of my entire self. I embraced the wise woman witch in me.

At this point of my life, I am deeply invested in growing wiser and learning how to use my love of the earth to grow, heal, and thrive. I know that my words are spells with creative power, and I move with a deliberate awareness of what I am sending out into the Creation. As I integrate all that I am learning, with attention and consistent practice, I grow my own book of secrets and shadows; this helps me know myself at a deeper and more profound level.

That is what a witch does. She facilitates balance and makes necessary adjustments in lockstep with the life that nature gave us. As I embrace being a witch, I can appreciate the gifts that Mama Gaia gives. It helps me to walk in gratitude, knowing how much I am really loved. It allows me to be right as rain and to stay harmonious, even in unharmonious times.

Besides being sustained by the love of the Divine, claiming my wise woman witchy self connects me to the knowledge and love of Mama Gaia, which sustains and nurtures me. The earth understands me and helps me to understand myself. She shares her gifts and magick with me, and I gratefully embrace that. Through our work, she grows in me. My grander self, the Divine Witch within, will never leave me.

Althea Grace

BUT YOU CAN'T STAY HERE

What do you do when you have a house guest who just won't go home? Nothing more than to magickally wish him away.

My friend, Amy, had a house guest... for months. I named him "Termite." He was a friend and business partner of Amy's husband who came to their home to work on a project. However, after the work was completed, he couldn't seem to find the front door.

One day Amy and three of our girlfriends were hanging out at my house. It had been evident, as soon as Amy walked in, that she was exasperated. I guess if someone had been burrowing into my rather comfy and somewhat expensive couch for week after week, I would be exasperated, too.

Amy felt that she shouldn't complain about it, and she sat with her arms tied in a knot and her toes bunched up in a ball. For the first time in all the years I had known her, she had nothing to say.

Now we couldn't have that. So, with a little coaxing, Amy's jaw unlocked and she began to speak about her squatter.

"It's not that Termite is not a nice guy, but the flippin' project is over," Amy said, her voice beginning to elevate. "He's been here for almost four months! I want my house back... I want my beautiful sofa back... I want to be able to walk around in my drawers! And who do you think is feeding him? I'm sure *Termite* would have been long gone if he had to pay a hotel bill."

Amy raised her eyes to look at the four of us individually and then said, "And my husband's not gettin' any, because he doesn't know how to tell his friend to leave." Amy was on a roll.

After we had all shared two large bowls of guacamole and copious amounts of soothing hibiscus-ginger-peach tea, Amy started to slow down. She groaned, "I just want him to go home."

Ha! I saw an opening and cut in. "Do you really care where he goes after he leaves your house? As the saying goes, you ain't gotta go home, but you can't stay here."

She cut me off. "No! I don't care where he goes." Termite had certainly tap danced on Amy's last nerve.

I sat back, crossed my legs, fingered the shiny silver heart dangling around my neck... and said, "In that case, are you up for a little woo-woo?"

Amy was all in.

She fired off a barrage of questions. She wanted to know when and where and what she needed to do, how soon it could be done, if we could all do it together, and what she needed to bring.

"Does the moon need to be in a certain place?"

I smiled and said, "You're watching too much TV. The moon is right where she needs to be... and so are you. Whatever phase the moon is in, if we need her, I'm sure she'll still help us out. We're going to do this right now."

First, I needed some basic info, like Termite's real name. Then we all needed to create an affirmation that wished Termite well and saw him happy but gone from Amy's home and out of her hair. After we had crafted a statement specifically for Amy's situation, it was time to get to work.

We had to open the way, so we said a prayer of peace and protection. We set an intention that this "work" would be for the good of all, harming none.

Once we were all grounded, I asked that we all stand up and face west. Why west? Cause the pendulum *said* to face west… of course.

Amy was then ready to say her affirmation out loud. We followed with all of us imagining Termite, happy as a clam, in a big, beautiful, glowing pink bubble of love suspended in the air.

Once everyone had this vision, I said, "On the count of three, let's just imagine that we are blowing this beautiful bubble, with Termite in it, out of Amy's house."

I asked everyone to picture the pink ball floating up into a clear blue sky until it was far, far away, and completely out of sight. We all did. I could see Amy begin to relax as she visualized the balloon slowly disappear.

However, I realized that seeing Termite well, happy, and gone was not enough. We needed to make sure this wouldn't happen again.

"Okay," I said, "now let's read the fine print on the warning label. It's important for you, Amy dear, to remember that when you and your husband are saying goodbye to Termite, and he is thanking you profusely for your hospitality, you are to just say 'Thank you.' If it gets awkward, you can add the 'Aww…You are just so sweet.' But do *not*, for any reason, say 'It's been a pleasure having you. Come back any time.' That will be the kiss of death."

"You don't have to tell me twice!" Amy said.

"Because if you add 'Come back anytime,' he *will* come back."

Amy made a joke about Termite turning around in the doorway, walking right back into her house, and plopping himself on her couch. Then the crew jumped in with more Termite jokes. We all ended up laughing and celebrating his departure by dancing a Termite-is-gone Conga line.

Finally, Amy asked, "Should I tell my husband?"

"I don't think so," I said. "This is woman's work. And anyway, it's done! Now just let the situation go, the same way you let go of that pink bubble. And until Termite stops lounging in your living room, any time you think about him, imagine the pink bubble floating away… or, if you like, picture an image of him, suitcase in hand, as he walks away from your house. If that's not enough, imagine his ass in a cab and you waving goodbye to him."

"I can do that," she said.

"Just hold the vision for a few seconds and move on before the image gets swampy. Always picture him with a smile on his face. Keep one on yours. Then move on. Otherwise, you'll get angry and stuck in 'When is he going?' instead of 'Yay! He's gone!'"

"How long will this take?" she asked eagerly.

"Termite will be out of your house in about a month, maybe less."

With that, we closed the circle with a prayer of gratitude for all seen and unseen assistance and left the issue of Amy's permanent house guest alone.

And Termite? Well, I have no idea why I said he would be out of Amy's house in less than a month—all I know is that he was!

Kmur Hardeman

I AM A WITCH

What does the word "witch" mean? So many stigmas are associated with it. I used to fear and deny this word, thinking, "If I am a witch, then I am going to hell."

But I had to face facts: A witch is exactly who I am.

Such acceptance did not come easy. I began my spiritual search in high school and my investigation became more intense during college. *Who was God? Was it just one male character?*

I looked through history, from the Egyptians to the Greeks and finally to the Celtic empires. I fell in love with it all, the history and uncovering that lost knowledge. I began watching everything I could on the Discovery and History channels. Somehow, it never clicked that the religions of that time could be something still valid in the present. I felt lost, searching and hungry for the possibilities of the ancient past.

God became real and more accessible when I stopped thinking of him as someone on high, judging us all. This was when I learned about Wicca, casting circles, and creating spells. I first heard the motto: "An ye harm none, do what ye will."

As I got caught up in the whirlwind of information, I perceived two gods—Mother Earth and the Horned One. These two conducted a dance of life, death, and rebirth that reflected the changes of seasons I honored.

I learned of the moon's special pull on those who practice magick. *Wicca* was a safe, if new, word. It seemed less volatile than that dreaded word *witch*—or so I thought. In Wicca, I could hide who I was. Wicca emphasized individual responsibility and self-imposed consequences, so I could enjoy the new experiences of my spiritual exploration without offending my family.

After graduating from college, I went back home, where it became obvious that there was no hiding for me. I erected a small altar that included candles representing the masculine and feminine, the God and the Goddess. The Bible still called to me on occasions—but how could one reconcile a double belief system? After all, the Bible told us, "Have no other Gods before me."

Was I being tempted? It felt like too much and not enough. As my search continued, ancient history kept luring me.

Then Isis made herself known. The most ancient of magick called to me from Egypt, the home of my African ancestors. Ceremonial magick appealed because it held more structure. There was no playing around now. It required a commitment to the triad: mother, father, and child instead of Father, Son, and Holy Spirit. From this, I perceived a sense of balance—not one, not two, but *three*. I felt a calling of spirit and a deeper understanding and awareness.

I enrolled in nursing school. Once I became a registered nurse, I started working in a hospital, where I noticed that the patients were segmented into conditions and body parts that need to be treated. Medicine's focus was alleviating symptoms and using medication to address their issues. I reacted with a deep inner turmoil.

Soon, I could no longer justify taking part in this kind of medicine. It did not feel right. We are more than separate body parts that need to be treated by different specialties. My inner unrest became reflected in the outside world.

This shouldn't have come as a surprise, based on the conflicting thoughts and different paths I'd studied in my long and complicated spiritual journey.

I was dissatisfied and continued searching for a "religion" that would work for me. I felt I needed a religion to take the place of another, so that I could settle my mind and resolve the beliefs of the past. I now had Isis, Osiris, and Horus—a triad—but I still had much to learn. For a few years, I dedicated myself to Isis and became a solitary practitioner. I tried to claim the Egyptian gods as my own, using books, rituals, and instincts.

Still wanting to make a difference in people's lives, I returned to school. I was interested in medicine but looking for a field of study that treats the whole person. Oriental medicine—was that the one? Yes, it was.

Oriental medicine is a balanced system that connected the symptoms to the organs and meridians that transect the entire body in a network of interconnecting parts, like a spider's web. The aim of treatments is to bring everything back into balance through acupuncture, herbs, massage, and for those interested, low-impact martial arts. Taking the leap, I became a doctor of Oriental medicine. My practice involved healing the energies of the body by reducing excesses and tonifying deficiencies.

My process for diagnosing and healing was drastically different from western medicine. For example, in Oriental medicine, the treatment for mental health is anchoring the spirit and clearing the heart. Everything counts. Mental health is not just "in your head," although many patients who cannot resolve their issues through western methods will be told this. My new healing modality encompassed all, honored all, and recognized the individual as one unit: body, mind, and spirit.

I now had magick on two planes of existence. What I could do with just an acupuncture needle was a type of magick—because what is magick if not manipulating the surrounding energy? With acupuncture and Oriental medicine, I could treat individual beings, creating miracles that rebalanced the body and let it heal itself of dis-harmonies.

I was even able to experience spiritual harmony with rituals and the Egyptian mysteries as I happily worked as an acupuncture physician, using multiple healing modalities.

Then I got sick, extremely sick. I received a death sentence.

Where had I gone wrong?

And so, a new journey began. It was slow, long, and painful. I had to stay hyper-focused just on survival. After eight months of chemo, my hair was gone and my life had become vomiting, bone pain, loss of appetite, and frailty. Yet surprisingly, the magick happened to me.

I went to the place where Source endured, vast and unquantifiable: the healing waters of the cosmos, where nothing and everything is. Where the mother, the father... no! Where the *All* held me close and love remained unconditional. I felt at home there.

Getting to that place was an act of desperation. It required traveling deep within, where the soul was no longer with the body, even as I remained on this plane of existence. Lying in a hospital bed, with machines beeping around me like a dull white noise, I pondered life and death. *Had I completed everything I was here to do? Was this enough, or was there more?*

Tears came but did not fall as I gave words to my fears: *If I go, those who love me, whose life connections are soul connections, will soon follow.* That, I could not allow. It was time for me to go where others could not pursue me. I needed help. Source awaited.

Eyes closed, I took a deep, slow, and steady breath. I descended. Taking deeper and longer breaths, I went further inward, repeating the process again and again. I awoke to find a moonlit sky above me, a darkened forest below, and an exceptionally long way to fall.

And then I fell, into the middle of shadows, trees, and silence. I knew I had a lengthy walk ahead.

Following instinct, I kept going. Finally, the silence ended. I heard the crash of waves on large rocks pulling me closer. I beheld a beach bathed in the full moon's light. No one else was around. I saw the sand taken over by the ocean with the continued push-pull of the waves. Behind an outcropping of forest, I saw a cave that seemed dark and mystical against the sky's glow.

It was time to dive deep into the unknown. Walking closer, I heard the crunching of sand underneath my feet change into soft footfalls on solid rock. I steeled myself and entered the cave. Shadows played on the walls, pale figures with luminescent shapes. Farther into the darkness I went.

Firelight flared out of nowhere. Looking around, I realized it was light from a torch, and less than three feet ahead of me I noticed stairs going down farther than the light can illuminate. With a quickened heartbeat, I descended the stairs, downward and deeper, the steps spiraling ever lower into darkness.

When the stairs ended, I stood on a flat, smooth surface in a rounded cavern. A muted light illuminated the space. Above me, the stalactites glowed, giving off light like distant stars. In front of me was a body of water so dark, it looked like liquid tar.

I took off my clothes—I was wearing a white robe—and stepped into the lake. My feet were covered first, then my knees, waist, and chest. Finally, I stood in water up to my neck. With the accelerated pitter-patter of my heart, I pushed off and began swimming until I reached the very center of the rounded cave.

I saw light above and darkness below. I gazed up and spread out like a starfish, relaxing. As I began to sink, I could no longer see the soft glow of the cave ceiling. Instead, I saw muddy reflections. Taking another breath and sinking deeper into nothingness, I let go. I felt nothing, heard nothing, and knew nothing. I became one with the void.

Time passed, but I couldn't tell how long. Suddenly, I awakened to the sound of a frightened voice calling my name. Someone was shaking me.

"What's going on?" I asked.

"You would not wake up," someone said. "You were barely breathing."

I remembered going to a place on a path seldom taken by the living.

"I was just meditating," I said with a smile. A burden had been lifted from me that day. I was no longer in survival mode.

I survived. I have encountered death from time to time throughout my life, and when I do, I feel no fear, knowing we shall all face it one day. While I was searching for a coven I could connect to, Hekate called to me. Being solitary was no longer satisfactory. I needed a community of like-minded people.

The Temple of Hekate became my home and the next chapter of my spiritual foundation. Hekate was the second goddess I dedicated myself to, the goddess of liminal places, torches, caves, and crossroads. This was not a coincidence.

I would call upon her when encountering death with families and friends, asking for her to ease their suffering and allow the dying to transition when it was their time. Within hours, I would hear of their passing. Was this good or bad? *Neither*, I would think. I now possessed a type of magick that was more connected. As a result, I was less afraid of walking my own path.

I realized now how mystical that moment was and how it had shaped me. Through an act of desperation, I had called for help. My answers had come from God. I knew now I could never be alone or abandoned.

This time of death, transformation, and rebirth shifted into my soul's journey. It laid the foundation from which I can call myself a witch.

My studies will continue. I am always learning and expanding my spiritual knowledge. I have become a witch of liminal places, born of joy, pain, loss, and exploration. That's where my magick comes from. It's who I am.

May your spiritual journey lead you home.

Enchanted Healer

BY FIRE BY FORCE

"You know you are more powerful than these men put together," the medicine man said.

I winced at the words. One doesn't commit to spiritual work to obtain power. I chose a question as my reply. "Is that why they fear me?"

I could sense them leering from a distance, the way a deer senses danger in the woods.

"Those with something to hide fear the ones who can see what's hidden," he answered. "If you weave stories with threads of untruths, you don't want the presence of someone with the power to unravel your lies."

Then he added a few more mystical words. "Most of the time, a bird is just a bird. That hawk is not just a bird. He's a messenger, your helper."

The hawk will have me see things through, I thought. *Like it or not*. It's the kind of medicine that has you feel the fear and do it anyway, for a higher good—even when I doubt my place in the world or I sense the difficulty ahead. In this case, it was a reference to my vision about fasting, despite the discomfort that my presence caused certain insecure men.

Dusk, the in-between time when the veil thins, is my favorite time of day. You can almost hear your ancestors' voices carried on the winds. I sat under a porch facing a distressed wooden fence, reflecting upon the weight of responsibility that comes with a vision. I wondered what the men experience on their vision quests.

Suddenly, I was startled as a screeching hawk flew under the porch, skimmed my head, and landed on the fence.

Without giving it much thought, I found myself standing near the bird. It cocked its head to look at me. We gazed, eye to eye. After what felt like ages, I blinked, and the moment and hawk vanished—but not before I was able to catch a glimpse of my reflection in the messenger's eye.

This is it. I had asked spirit for clarity and had received the very symbol of vision. I could no longer ignore the magnetic pull of my call to fast for four days, embrace my path, and share my visions.

Each day of my four-day fasting commitment, I was visited by a hawk. On the fourth and final morning, it gifted me with a feather, as if to say, "This was no dream."

For four nights, I was also visited by an owl. It became my eyes and ears during the pitch dark and lively desert nights. Owl continues to be my eyes and ears through times of darkness and instability. To this day, my prophetic dreams are sometimes accompanied by alarming owl shrieks. The bird's call signals the urgency with which spirit is trying to get through to me. This can be jarring, exhausting, and lonesome. When you have a vision, you really live through it twice—once as a vision or dream, and again as it unfolds in waking life. Sometimes, the most urgent messages are not received well… or not received at all.

I remembered the medicine man's words later, as I struggled with a foreboding vision.

Dreams, even the daydreams that seem more like nightmares, disturb our peace. Those vivid images were often followed by an owl screeching... no, *screaming*, just outside the window.

"You paranoid city girl," my husband teased.

Because I've never lived in such isolation, my husband was quick to pass off my most disturbing dream as the fear and paranoia of a city slicker.

"But I didn't just see fire this time," I pleaded with him. "I dreamt of firetrucks ripping up the dirt road while the neighbors recklessly hauled the horse trailer downhill in the other direction. I could feel the heat coming off the flames. I know what I know!" By then, I was shouting.

My ears were still ringing from the sirens in my dreams—but nobody believed me. I felt utterly defeated as I sank deeper into the armchair. In that moment, I was more isolated than ever. *Will it always be like this? Am I ignored for being a woman?*

My grandma was a *curandera*. Surely, there's ancestral trauma that I need to heal. *Let's not go down that rabbit hole! All sensitives probably experience this.* It's just human frailty to fear that accepting Spirit's warnings means we cosign on said tragedy.

Rather than let devastation consume me, I leaned into my intuition and trusted in Spirit. Reaching for my medicines, I began praying for protection. I laid down a line of protection around the house, as I do whenever I feel anxiety coursing through my body, while I waited to see if my dream premonition became a reality.

Due to scheduled rolling blackouts, our power was out. The generator ran thunderously as it operated the air conditioner, my only reprieve from the windy October scorchers.

The generator's roar made the helicopters inaudible.

The neighbor tore up my driveway, honking and yelling at me to evacuate. I shoved clothes into a bag and loaded the dog into the jeep. There was only one way in and out of my neighborhood: an unpaved dirt road. I raced toward the billowing black cloud that looked like something out of a horror film.

Later that evening, we watched in terror and awe as our property burned on live television. The flames engulfed everything up to the protection barrier I had laid down but left our house intact. Under the cover of night, we snuck onto our property to extinguish a few spot fires. With no city plumbing connection and no streetlights, we fumbled about with buckets from our water tank, dousing the hot, orange embers that sprang up from a black void.

My ears strained to hear owls, but all I heard was the ground sizzle, whispering secrets. The embers stirred, kicking up a memory of a dark sweat lodge when I listened to the grandpas gurgle and speak as water was poured over them.

I am safe on this part of the journey. I take heart. For all my suffering and questioning my sanity, I now see the bigger picture and accept all the parts that make the whole. This has been the conduit to accepting all parts of myself.

I can't make others accept my visions, but I can humbly take heed when Spirit speaks.

Eva Galindo

GOD'S WITCH

The light in the church shone softly on her beautiful blue dress. I stared at her lying in the coffin. Someone picked me up and leaned me forward so I could kiss her hard, cold cheek.

Suddenly a shift happened, as if a camera was rolling pictures before my eyes. New Edition was playing on the radio as I watched my second-oldest brother staring at her obituary. Tears rolled down his face. Our oldest brother raced over to hug him, and I crawled into the arms of them both. Their hurt was so deep, I could feel it as my own.

I was four years old when my mother passed away. By the time I was in the third grade, I couldn't remember her alive, but I never forgot her funeral. I was sent to live with my aunt and uncle that year. It was the loneliest feeling. My oldest brother had moved out at age sixteen, and the second oldest was sent to live with his dad. They left me alone in a completely unknown place.

At night, when I lay down to sleep, an overwhelming urge would pull me out of bed and over to the window in my room. Peering through the burglar bars, I would look into the sky. The moon was always so beautiful. I would talk to her about everything because she was the only mother I knew.

Every day after school, I would go to the patio window of the den and say, "I want my brother!" repeatedly. I cried as I imagined him coming up the street.

One day as I was going through my routine at the window, my brother appeared! I wiped my tears, flew to the side door, and pretended nothing was wrong as I leaped into his arms for his hugs. He was my superhero. I knew my words had brought him to me.

I learned to pray on my knees by watching my aunt and uncle every night. They were Catholic. I learned the Lord's Prayer at a Catholic church we attended every Sunday. The smell of the incense and taste of the wine was compelling. One night, as I prayed on my knees to God, I asked him if I could be a witch—but not just any witch. I wanted to be *His* witch, so I could help people and heal them. Instead, I learned to heal myself.

Sitting in my first ritual circle, I felt a battle between my worlds. *If she says anything about the devil, I'm out of here,* I thought.

"Sweet Jesus," she said.

My heart stopped pounding and I was full of comfort and acceptance. I found that witches are real and there are others just like me: people who believe in God and practice witchcraft. The battle between my worlds and myself was won.

So much time has passed, and I have learned that my identity is witch, and my religion is Christianity.

I'm a witch. God's Witch.

Cherkesha Sylvinnie Caesar

THE WAND CHOOSES THE WITCH

*M*any, many years ago, when I was first stumbling on the path of being a witch, I didn't have any of the accoutrements witches have. I didn't have crystals or a wand, and I didn't know where to get such things. I was overwhelmed. I was exiting Christianity, and it was a difficult period for me.

I felt laden with judgment, and I was terrified to wade into the witchy waters. As a former fundamentalist Christian—I had spent twenty-six years in the cult of Jehovah's Witnesses—these thoughts plagued me. I didn't know if my soul was going to the dark side or if the devil was trying to get me.

As a witch now, I get to live a life of absolute freedom. I can write books about witchcraft and about being on my path as a witch and offering what I can to the global conversation on witches. I especially love dispelling myths and misconceptions that people have about witches.

However, it was not always so. My mind was in a vastly different place back then.

During this period of my life, I didn't know where to go to learn. I devoured the few books I could find on magick and witchcraft.

Though I'm happily divorced now, at the time, I was still married to my Baptist husband, the perfect healing partner. I'm forever grateful for him.

One summer, during a vacation to Arizona, we went to a beautiful spa: Miraval Spa in Tucson. It was unlike any spa I'd seen. I loved it there, especially gazing up at the stars in the pitch black at night. Without light pollution, the stars could be seen in a canopy above my head.

We also visited the Grand Canyon. As I approached the north rim, tears welled up and rolled down my cheeks. I was in awe. Spending time in nature at the spa and at the Grand Canyon turned up the volume of my inner witch.

During the trip, I received an intuitive urge to go to Sedona. While we were near the Grand Canyon, I saw signs that said "Sedona." I took it as a metaphysical sign. I'd never been to that city, yet I felt an irresistible calling to go there. I had no idea why.

Our next stop was Phoenix, to visit friends for a few days before flying home from Phoenix airport. During the short visit to Phoenix, I announced to my husband and friends that I wanted to go to Sedona.

"Oh, that's a long drive from here," they said, adding that it wasn't practical to try to make that kind of side trip. "Next time you come, we'll all go."

But that didn't work for me. My inner witch was insistent, saying "Sedona." The urge to go there almost felt like a compulsion. I couldn't stop talking about it.

My husband asked me a point-blank question I couldn't answer: "You have to go to Sedona for *what?*"

"I don't know. I just have to get there."

He looked at me like I had three heads.

But I knew there must be a reason why I kept hearing this word, and I knew I would do everything in my power to answer the call.

My husband and friends represented the out-picturing of my inner voices, which questioned my intuitive knowing. *Why are you going there? For what? There's nobody you know there anyway.*

Besides, we were flying out of Phoenix at 1:30 Saturday afternoon. We'd have to be at the airport by noon at the latest.

Because my husband was not on the same page as me, this was a journey I would make alone. I let everyone know on Friday night.

"I've looked it up and mapped it out," I announced. "I'm leaving for Sedona at five a.m. in the rental car. I'll be back in time for us to get on our plane."

Now they were *all* looking at me like I had three heads.

I awoke at four the next morning and went into stealth mode, dressing in the dark, with one thing on my mind: getting to Sedona. As I started my drive, I felt good, accomplished, and happy. I drove through what they call the Green Valley, praying, playing music, and feeling alive. As I continued driving, I finally came to the point on the route where the red rock starts to show itself. Both the landscape and the energy changed the closer I got to Sedona.

Suddenly, I was in this beautiful vortex of energy. As I entered Sedona and saw Bell Rock, I realized in my spirit that I was home. Everything seemed somehow familiar. I felt a *yes* in my spirit.

I was at the famed Bell Rock, a place people visit from all over the world. Many have traveled far to sit on this rock, experience its vortex energy, and walk around its circumference.

I still didn't know where I was going. My inner knowing was my only guide. I arrived at a circle and something told me to go right. I went right. It felt right.

The vibration was wonderful, delicious, and Divine. I felt things happening in my body and consciousness. *I could hang out here for a really long time.*

Then my mind remembered that I had a plane to catch.

I made the right onto Chapel Road and saw a church jutting out of the side of a mountain. It beckoned to me: "Come." I had never seen anything like this.

As I entered the Chapel of the Holy Cross, I felt serene, warm, and bathed in the glow of candles that visitors had lit for their loved ones.

Straight ahead, I saw a huge cross. For me, a cross is a sign of death. It symbolizes the willing death of the physical, lower nature, which we choose to give up so we can ascend to the highest aspect of consciousness.

I'm from a Christian background and I love churches. I've visited holy houses all over the world. At the time, I did not know that I was going to become a practicing Christian Witch. That path was still unfolding.

I knew that the chapel was likely sitting on some kind of vortex of ancient energy, so I sank down on one of the pews and closed my eyes in deep thankfulness that I'd made the journey. Tears streamed down my face, but I didn't know why. I was overcome. The energy around me was amazing, and as I sat there, I felt an opening and things just falling away. I couldn't put into words what was going on inside me, but I knew it was miraculous and unlike anything I'd ever experienced.

I don't know how long I sat there; It could have been two hours or ten hours. Time stood still. I went so deep into meditation that when I came to, everything was different: my body, my mind, and even my emotions.

Periodically, I would open my eyes and see people coming and going. Then I'd close my eyes again, falling deeper into meditation. More tears. I breathed and let it all happen, and it was delicious.

When I felt complete with that experience, I got up, having no idea what time it was. I didn't have a watch. The voice within me said, "Come downstairs." The beckoning was not done with me. I didn't know what was downstairs, yet I went.

I found a store. I was not all the way back to full conscious awareness, still having the experience I'd had on the church pew. I could feel that I was not fully in my body.

I walked up and down the aisles slowly, looking around. Before this trip to Arizona, I had been reading and studying about the craft of magick. I didn't have a wand. I had read in a wisdom book that "the wand chooses you," and you know when it happens.

Reading that, I was full of questions. *How could a wand choose me? Would I walk by a wand on the street and watch it hop up on me? How could it find me?*

As I walked through the store, the thought came to me about the wand— but nothing here resembled one. This was a Christian store in a Catholic church. They wouldn't carry wands here, even in Sedona, where virtually every spiritual and magickal implement can be found.

Valerie, you're not finding a wand in here, I thought to myself.

I tried to stay open, walking up and down the aisles, when something told me to stop and look down. I saw the wand. I didn't touch it, at first. I just stood there staring at it. Finally, I lifted the box that the wand was in. It was resting on the white, fluffy filling inside the box. It was as if it had jumped on me. The spirit of this wand had chosen me and said, *Pick me up. I'm yours.*

And when I saw it, I said to myself, *This is my wand.*

My wand was an eight-inch-long nail with one simple word engraved on it: "Forgiven."

That nail became my first wand as a practicing Christian Witch. I've wrought powerful magick with that wand, and I have it to this day.

Its message was that I didn't have to carry guilt or shame or fear. I didn't need to be afraid of my path, wherever it might lead. Many times in the years that followed, I waved the "Forgiven" nail wand over myself.

Few things have affected a change in my life like forgiveness and love. Love and forgiveness are a couple. The fullest expression of love is only possible when you know that you are forgiven and when you have forgiven everyone for everything. Love is only fully expressed when there is nothing in the way.

My wand reminds me that everything has been forgiven. That's how my wand found me.

And yes, I missed my flight—but I gained my magick.

Valerie Love

PART THREE

*Deepening Your Relationship
with the Witch*

A witch ought never to be frightened in the darkest forest because she should be sure in her soul that the most terrifying thing in the forest was her.

— TERRY PRATCHETT

HONORING THE ELEMENTS AND CELESTIAL CYCLES

———•———•———•———

*E*xploring the realm of the witch through action and expression affords deeper insight into this archetype who defies definition. A powerful witch is in alignment with the elements, energies, and cycles of nature.

A witch is an empowered being who does not seek or ask for approval or permission. She is an initiator of her entire life experience and might even be in the business of helping others do likewise. An inherent aspect of the witch is about activating, cultivating, expanding, and using power. A powerful witch acts as a force beyond comprehension and is not acted upon.

What is the source of the witch's power? This varies from witch to witch. All power is sourced from the pure field of consciousness that could be referred to as the Divine. Everything in the universe is from the same Divine source, and therefore all witches draw power from the same place—but not all witches use the same conduits of Divine energy to power their life and craft. The Divine is all. This source can be channeled in a myriad of ways and can appear in an infinite array of forms.

THE ELEMENTS

Divine energy can be channeled through and as the elements of earth, air, fire, and water. While these four elements represent the building blocks of everything in manifest reality, the fifth element, *ether*, represents the spirit realm. It is important to note that modern science agrees with the witch in its assertion that there are four states of matter: solids (earth), gas (air), plasma (fire), and liquid (water).

Examination of the elements gives us a glimpse into the operation of the witch and how these may be used to heal and transform.

EARTH

Characteristics and aspects of the element of earth include:

- Grounding
- Stabilizing
- Supporting
- Rooting

Items the witch uses to represent the element of earth include:

- Crystals
- Stones and rocks
- Precious metals
- Soil
- Ash
- Sand
- Salt

Earth is the foundation for the other three elements: air, fire, and water. Without earth, these could not exist. Earth is represented in the Tarot as the suit of Pentacles, pertaining to the physical body, real estate, possessions, money, and everything in the material realm.

Vegetation, plants, and flowers that represent the energy of earth are root vegetables, including beets, potatoes, turnips, carrots, and bulbs that grow in the earth.

The witch calls upon the element of earth, when appropriate, to ground and root situations. This example from my life experience might help to explain the use of earth as a powerful ally.

Many years ago, after I'd left my career as a financial planner to embark on being a teacher of spirituality, I experienced a dramatic decline in income. Because I had not yet become adept at generating significant income in the realm of human transformation, I experienced countless financial setbacks, increased debt, and even losing a home. While this was all part of my personal curriculum in service of my ascension, it was painful at the time. I felt unmoored and unstable, as if a strong gust of wind could carry me anywhere it desired, whether I wanted to go or not. Something had to be done. I needed to create greater financial abundance as a steady stream of income, and I also needed a way of settling into a home and feeling grounded.

I employed earth magick for the win. I began a practice of rooting into our Earth Mother in my meditations and drawing up veritable boulders of the energy into my being. I envisioned myself as stable, planted, and in a beautiful home that was secure, financially and otherwise. It's not easy to answer the call of destiny while feeling as if one is an ever-turning leaf in the wind. This was especially challenging for me because I relate closely with the element of air and am an air sign. To change the energy and flavor of my life during that tumultuous season, I had to tap into energies beyond air. I had to root into earth.

Earth magick grounded me and my energy, affording a firmer foundation on which to build. This was primarily achieved with the help of the crystal kingdom, and particularly the harder stones in the quartz family, including:

- A tiger's eye crystal I wore as a necklace to serve as a *talisman* for grounding and centering. A talisman is an object that can be worn that carries a specific magickal intention. My intention was to ground and root myself and give my life a firm foundation.

- Pink quartz crystal, which I procured in copious amounts and placed on altars in whatever space I found myself. I also carried this crystal in my purse and pockets. The crystal rooted me in love, the most powerful force in the universe.

- Purple amethyst served me well in all my full-moon Tarot readings on why my life was unfolding as it was, what I specifically needed to change and by when, and what people and situations were problematic and which were beneficial. Purple amethyst remains one of my all-time favorite crystals for clear perception in spirit realms and was therefore twice blessed for both grounding me and affording me access to higher wisdom.

- At the top of my list of favorite crystals, because of its comprehensive healing properties, is clear quartz crystal. This is also among the hardest of stones, thus making it a perfect ally for earth magick. My clear quartz crystals were used on the altar, in readings, and on the tip of a magick wand I use to direct energy.

I'm happy to state that the magickal workings yielded extraordinary fruit in the way of increased income and a beautiful home. Of course, spiritual work alone is not sufficient to change one's life in a dramatic fashion. Taking a holistic approach to the elements means working with their physical counterparts as well as their spiritual energies. While I was doing spell work with the element of earth, I also had to write books that would provide ongoing royalties; run a profitable business by acquiring clients; and become friendly with the energy of money. These are all earth-based pursuits. If I hadn't applied both magick and practical effort, I would not have achieved the results I desired.

AIR

Characteristics and aspects of the element of air include:

- Uplifting
- Inspiring
- Swift moving
- Clearing

Items the witch uses to represent the element of air include:

- Representations of birds and butterflies
- Feathers and wings
- Wands
- Fans
- Bells
- Incense
- Brooms and *besoms*, a broom made with natural materials such as twigs and/or branches
- Swords and *athames*, a dagger or knife used in witchcraft

The element of air is represented in the Tarot as swords and is the most problematic of all four of the suits in the book of Tarot, because it encompasses the power of negative thoughts to derail us. As a representation of the witch's mental faculties, the element of air fosters a clear mind and the ability to think critically. A witch must be able to communicate clearly in spell work and incantations, to optimize potential for changing the self and the world.

Witches who are intimately connected with and work with the element of air can call on these powers:

- A strong mental prowess that is required to understand correspondences used in spell work and to set powerful intentions, along with the mental fortitude to see them through to fruition, even when the task at hand becomes difficult and the urge to abandon the project arises. It takes a mentally strong witch to stay powerfully focused on spell work until the results are seen in the physical dimension.
- The ability to outsmart opponents as if in a game of chess, while remembering all opponents are not external. Thinking steps ahead is an unmistakable sign of the element of air.
- The ability to debate and argue a position to influence outcomes. The witch does this in physical reality as well as in dimensions of consciousness beyond this world by communicating with spirits in a compelling fashion, so that they lend their aid to the witch.

FIRE

Characteristics and aspects of the element of fire include:

- Energizing
- Vivifying
- Purifying
- Purging

Items the witch uses to represent the element of fire include:

- Fire itself, controlled indoors in a hearth or fireplace, or in an outdoor fire pit
- Candles
- Cauldrons

- Wands
- The sun

The element of fire is represented in the Tarot as the suit of wands, describing the spiritual aspect of self. Fire energizes and purges, as is illustrated in the forest, a natural domain of the witch. Even as devastating fire sweeps through the forest, we remember that all is not destroyed. Fire eats dead and decaying underbrush, leaves, and plant material, releasing nutrients into the soil that aid biodiversity while simultaneously checking species of plants that are growing out of control to the detriment of surrounding plant species.

The wisdom of fire in the wild knows when to erupt; what to clear, cleanse, and purify; and what to activate, making way for the new and unborn. Fire knows when to burn itself out.

The witch honors fire with candles for the power to catalyze healing and transformation through sacred rituals and spell work. These candles are engraved with sacred symbols and sigils, dressed with appropriate essential oils and herbs, and then burned with a powerful intention. As the candle burns, the witch "reads" the fire by paying close attention to the action and duration of the flame. After the candle has been eliminated by the element of fire, the container is also "read" by examining the pattern of wax, smoke, and remaining debris to determine the efficacy and the chances that the candle worked.

Candle meditations on the sacred flame sharpen the mind, purify thoughts, and activate and engage the third eye for active vision beyond this world.

Each year in the autumn, many witches use the element of fire at the celebration of Samhain (sow-in), a sacred festival that falls on October 31. Originating as a Celtic celebration, Samhain is now observed by Wiccans, witches, and pagans in many traditions all over the world.

I attended an open Samhain festival each year for several years conducted by a Druid and three witches. In attendance were witches of divergent backgrounds and practices, all clad in full ceremonial regalia including crowns, cloaks, and wands. It was a most sacred ceremony, and fire played the central role. We burned away old hurts, disturbing memories, and haunts from the past year by writing these on paper and releasing them into the sacred flames. We allowed every vestige of negating energy that no longer served us to be consumed at the foot of the sacred, raging fire.

WATER

Characteristics and aspects of the element of water include:

- Flowing
- Cleansing
- Refreshing
- Satiating
- Nurturing

Items the witch uses to represent the element of water include:

- Water from a variety of sources for their energetic correspondences: rain, ocean, river, lake, pond, storm. While in Egypt, I sourced water for magickal purposes from the River Nile for its storied past, and the fact that it's one of the longest rivers in the world, supporting life for millions of people in several countries along its banks in Africa. This river water can be used for its ancient and modern properties of life sustenance.
- Ocean and sea items, including shells and fins
- Chalices and cups
- Symbols of the moon

The element of water is represented in the Tarot as cups and describes emotions and feelings. The well of life is the cauldron of the heart, out of which life expression flows as love, gratitude, joy, fulfillment, peace, and the full range of feelings and emotional expression we get to experience as spiritual, humanoid beings.

Where there's water, there's life. Amniotic fluid is similar in composition to ocean water; both contain salts essential for the life they harbor and nurture. Our similitude to our earth home does not end when we exit the amniotic sac. Our bodies are 70 percent water. We cannot survive without the element of water and all its sacred, life-sustaining gifts.

Beyond the physical properties and blessings of water, the witch engages the element of water, from its many sources, for spiritual and energetic purposes. A witch gathers rain for use in spells and rituals that call for nurturing and growth, and collects sea water to be used for ritual and spell work to bring about conditions of oceanic abundance. River water might be used for rituals and spell work that would cleanse the unwanted and wash it out of our lives.

Many years ago, I led a group in a ritual to release lack and limitation. Everyone in the group was suffering from some form of lack, and we'd had enough. The ritual contained several steps, including writing out on a piece of paper the exact conditions we were releasing. Then the paper was to be ripped into shreds, inserted into an envelope, and taken to the river for disposal.

At the edge of the river, we asked for the river's help in releasing us of this energetic waste. The river gave permission. I stepped closer to the edge and placed my envelope full of all the negative energies into the water and watched the enveloped float peacefully away. As I watched, something startling occurred. The envelope opened from the bottom, and all the tiny bits of paper were sucked out toward the bottom of the river. I felt a tremendous release.

While all the preparatory steps and items of the ritual had gotten us ready for this release, the culmination at the river's edge fomented the elimination we were so avidly seeking. I have never forgotten this ritual. As a witch, I align with the enduring power of water. Its energy is always nearby, as water surrounds us in copious amounts on this life-sustaining planet.

THE WITCH'S WHEEL OF THE YEAR

The Wheel of the Year as honored by witches and pagans across cultures is, at its essence, attuned to honoring the seasons and cycles.

While names of the seasons and cycles of the earth's dance around the sun vary, as do the practices of individual witches, the essence of these celebrations is honoring the earth and sun as aspects of nature that affect us all. As witches, we choose to deeply engage all seasons and cycles, and we use our rituals to find the bliss and joy in each season and cycle, whether it's a personal favorite or not.

I was born during the season of the Fall Equinox. I grew up in New York City, where the seasons were on full display, from trudging through snow drifts up to my hips to picking apples at an apple farm in upstate New York. The long car ride from the city gave us meditative experiences of every shade of red, orange, and yellow as the leaves turned into sentinels of the coming cold. Though fall and winter were significant for me growing up, spring and summer remain my favorite times of year. I do not favor winter, but as a witch, I honor this season for its gifts of darkness, replenishment, and hibernation, as well as its ability to still us in a quiet, serene blanket of pure white.

Not all witches engage the eight *sabbats* or celebrations of the Wheel of the Year, but it is a significant aspect of many witchcraft traditions and is important to solitary witches and secular witches alike.

THE SABBATS

Samhain (October 31-November 1): This festival, akin to Halloween, marks the end of the harvest season and the beginning of the dark half of the year. It is a time to honor the ancestors and the dead and to reflect on the cycles of life and death. Our Halloween customs of dressing in costumes and carving pumpkins have their roots in the festivals of Samhain. During this time, the veil between this world and the world of the dead is thin, and thus communication with spirits of those who have passed on becomes easier.

Yule (December 21-22): The winter solstice festival celebrates the rebirth of the sun and the return of the light. It is a time to gather with loved ones and to honor the sacredness of the earth. This ancient pagan festival is the forerunner to the modern-day Christmas, bringing many of its sacred customs along with it, including the yule log, mistletoe, feasting, gift-giving, and placing lights and ornaments on evergreen trees.

Imbolc (February 1-2): Also known as Candlemas, this festival marks the midpoint between the winter solstice and the spring equinox. It is a time to honor the goddess Brigid and to celebrate the coming of spring. Candlemas, being a Christian observance borrowed from pagan practices, features lighting candles and bonfires, as does Imbolc.

Ostara (March 20-21): The spring equinox festival celebrates the balance between light and dark and the renewal of life. It is a time to plant seeds and to honor the goddess Eostre. Easter, derived from the pagan celebration of Ostara, still bears much of the symbolism of the older festival. Both are celebrated at the time of the vernal equinox and are associated with rabbits or hares, the sacred totem of the goddess Eostre, and chicks and eggs to symbolize fertility and new life.

Beltane (May 1): This festival, also known as May Day, marks the beginning of summer and the fertility of the earth. It is a time to celebrate love and to honor the God and Goddess. In our modern day, the celebration of May Day has been influenced by both pagan and secular traditions. May Day is celebrated around the world as a holiday that honors workers and the labor movement. Celebrations incorporate ancient customs and rituals associated with Beltane, such as the maypole dance and the crowning of a May Queen.

Litha (June 20-21): The summer solstice festival celebrates the height of summer and the longest day of the year. It is a time to honor the Sun god and to celebrate abundance and growth.

Lammas (August 1): Also known as *Lughnasadh*, this festival marks the beginning of the harvest season. It is a time to give thanks for the bounty of the earth and to honor the god Lugh.

Mabon (September 21-22): The fall equinox festival celebrates the balance between light and dark, as well as the harvest season. It is a time to give thanks for the abundance of the earth and to honor the Goddess.

For witches who celebrate all eight sabbats, each festival is marked with its own practices, rituals, and symbols to honor the time of year and the cycles of the earth and sun that sustain our lives on this planet. Observance of the witch's Wheel of the Year has penetrated every area and strata of society, including religious circles. We do well to remember that the witch is alive and active in a host of our celebrations and customs, if only we dare to look.

THE SOLAR CYCLE

For witches who do not celebrate the Wheel of the Year as eight specific festivals, the practice of honoring the solstices and equinoxes is another ritualistic opportunity to align with the solar cycle. Religious witches and secular witches alike agree on the scientific truth that the earth revolves around the sun. There is an occult spiritual truth embedded in this cycle: humanity is influenced by the annual dance of the earth and sun. Witches honor the solar cycle and its effects upon all life on this planet. If it were not for the turning of the earth on its axis and its journey around the star of our galaxy, we would not be alive.

The solar cycle is marked at four points: the spring or vernal equinox, summer solstice, fall or autumnal equinox, and the winter solstice.

Our earth home is remarkable in that it not only rotates around the sun, but it is also tilted at 23.5 degrees, which creates the seasons. Add to this the earth's spin on its axis, and you have quite the cosmic dance indeed. When we consider that the earth is hurtling through space at 67,000 miles per hour in an elliptical orbit around the sun, while spinning at 1,000 miles per hour at the equator, while maintaining its tilt at a 23.5-degree angle, we have reason to be in awe.

A day marks the completion of a rotation of the earth, making each new day worthy of our welcoming. We have completed another perilous journey among the stars unscathed, which is more than enough reason to welcome every dawn.

The earth and sun dance is the kindling of our solar rituals as witches. It is fired by a deep awe of the natural world; reverential appreciation of our earth home and all it is doing in each moment; and the majesty that defies comprehension that we all participate in every day.

The four points of the earth's dance around the sun include two equinoxes and two solstices.

THE EQUINOXES

During the earth's orbit around the sun, twice per year the earth's axis is not tilted toward *or* away from the sun, yielding a homeostasis of sorts. These are the equinoxes, when day and night are equal. The witch honors the equanimity of darkness and light, day and night. These two co-existing powers are equal. Our equinox celebrations honor our recognition that we have the powers of both light and dark at our disposal. During both equinoxes, we attune our rituals, thoughts, and intentions to the perfect balance found in nature's ebb and flow. The rhythm and harmony of the cosmos as day and night perfectly match.

THE SOLSTICES

In the earth and sun dance, there are two times per year that the earth's tilt is fully toward the sun or away from the sun, depending on where you are located on this planet.

On the summer solstice, when the sun is high in the sky, positioned over the Tropic of Cancer, the greatest current of light is available to us on the longest day of the year.

On the winter solstice, the sun is positioned over the Tropic of Capricorn, revealing the least light and producing the longest night of the year.

THE FOUR POINTS OF THE YEAR

Examining each equinox and solstice more closely reveals the underpinning of our rituals during these cosmic events. These differ in the northern and southern hemispheres. A look at each of the four points as we move through the year serves as a compass for daily living, rituals, and spell work.

WINTER SOLSTICE

The winter solstice graces us annually in the northern hemisphere on December 21 or 22 and in the southern hemisphere on June 20 or 21.

The northern hemisphere will experience this as the shortest day and longest night of the year, while the southern hemisphere will experience the exact opposite: the longest day and shortest night of the year.

The winter solstice is a time of great remembrance and celebration around the world. It has become a point of connection between witches and seemingly distant spiritual paths, such as Christianity. There are cultural, religious, and historical connections between Christmas and the winter solstice. Christmas is celebrated on December 25, each year, which is close to the winter solstice in the northern hemisphere.

In times long ago, peoples of varying cultures and religions celebrated the winter solstice as a time of the return of the sun after a long, dark night. When winter enfolds us, the winter solstice reminds us that this, too, is temporary. Soon, the winter grip will loosen and release as spring bursts forth. The winter solstice is a harbinger of relief from the deathly cold of winter and a return to flowers, green grass, and new birth.

The early Christian church chose to celebrate the birth of Jesus Christ on a date that would align with the winter solstice, as it was already a time of great celebration to those living in the birthplace of Christianity's customs. Our forebears celebrated the winter solstice with vigor and passed their celebration on to billions of people in the form of Christmas, when lights fill our human habitations and many rejoice at the birth of the Son/Sun.

Every witch's celebration of the winter solstice will be unique, even if celebrating in a coven. Each witch is a unique phenomenon with the agency to "do as one wills." Even witches who choose to celebrate together in covens still honor their own majestic and unique observances.

In the mystery school I founded to teach esoteric and occult knowledge, initiations of new witches take place on the winter solstice after a long year of study. During the witching hour—between three and six a.m.—the initiates are whisked away to a secret location in nature where they endure the trials of initiation held as sacred and secret in our tradition. In the dark, still, cold night, with snow crunching underfoot, they die to the old and will be reborn with the sun.

The winter solstice is the epitome of deadness. This makes it an invitation to relax and be still, contemplate, reflect, and sink into the tomb of nature to hibernate. We allow the soil to rest and replenish. Nature unfolds in cycles, as do we. Winter primes us to understand death is not the enemy. It is a necessary transition and transmutation so that life can birth the new and keep all existence strumming along.

Just as death cannot exist without life, life cannot exist without death. Dead and decaying leaves on the forest floor illustrate the vital truth of an unbroken continuum of birth and death. Fallen foliage becomes an indispensable constituent of compost from which new trees spring forth. Awareness of the new life that will soon emerge from the dormant, long, cold nights of the winter season keeps us inspired and eager for spring's first blush and buds.

During the winter solstice, the witch leaves off strenuous activity and slips into a partial hibernation, naturally slowing down. We imagine a scene of blanket-clad bodies sipping hot cocoa by a fire, gazing out the window at snow drifts and barren trees standing in silence. A great, white hush has fallen on everything the eye can see, reminding us to still the mind and be silent within. The stillness is not void of action. There is a deeper action unfolding beneath the tundra. In the depths of the frozen earth, the activity of nature is preparing itself, yet again, for another spring.

The witch uses this cycle of death and rebirth to teach us the wisdom of nonattachment and the requirement to be still in that season. It is a reminder that death will always give way to new life, so we need not mourn without solace. This is the witch as a comforter, which is an often unnoticed and disregarded aspect of this ancient archetype.

SPRING EQUINOX

The spring or the vernal equinox occurs on March 20 or 21 when the earth's axis is neutral, which means the lengths of day and night will be equal in all parts of the world.

In the northern hemisphere, the spring equinox marks the beginning of spring, while in the southern hemisphere, it marks the beginning of autumn.

Witches welcome the spring equinox for its radiating and renewing energy and the surge of vitality and freshness in the air. We are energized, as everything around us has emerged from the dead silence of winter and burst into colorful buds and sprouts. Tiny green saplings push their way up through the earth, and we are reminded of the upward thrust we all must engage in to grow into our full potential. The energy of the spring equinox is renewal, rebirth, fresh beginnings, and revitalization.

Our rituals, at this point of the earth's journey around the sun, are focused on setting new intentions for the season, planting, and honoring fertility in all its aspects while the natural world is being bathed in pollen. While spring equinox rituals vary widely from witch to witch, there are themes and commonalities. On the spring equinox, witches will tend to engage in:

> **Spring cleaning**: Many witches view the spring equinox as a time for purification and renewal. We may perform a spring cleaning ritual to clear out any negative or stagnant energy in our homes or sacred spaces. Mom taught us spring cleaning, and even administered potions for us to cleanse the colon seasonally.

> **Egg decorating**: Eggs are a symbol of fertility and new beginnings, and many witches decorate eggs as part of their spring equinox celebrations. This can involve painting or dyeing eggs with natural materials or creating intricate designs and symbols. Though these have all been borrowed by Christians to create Easter, they remain in the witch's seasonal celebrations.

Planting seeds: The spring equinox is a time when the natural world awakens from the long, dark, and cold winter night, and comes to life. Witches who garden and tend the earth will plant seeds along with intentions for the coming year.

Honoring the goddess Ostara: Some witches may honor the goddess Ostara, who is associated with the spring equinox, through offerings, prayers, or rituals. In some traditions, Ostara is syncretized with the Greek goddess Persephone, who represents the cycle of death and rebirth as she spends part of the year in the underworld and part of the year above ground. Likewise, Ostara is a goddess of resurrection and new beginnings, who brings the light and fertility of spring to the world after the darkness of winter.

The spring equinox is a time of renewal, growth, and new beginnings, and the witch will celebrate this point of the year by connecting with the natural world's rebirth and resurgence from seeming death.

SUMMER SOLSTICE

The summer solstice occurs on June 20 or 21, when the earth's tilt is toward the sun, producing the longest day of the year in the northern hemisphere, with access to the greatest light, while producing the longest night of the year in the southern hemisphere, affording access to darkness.

Summer solstice rituals of the witch afford the opportunity to honor the heat and fire of the sun, represented as bonfires or campfires. We celebrate growth in full bloom, the verdant outcome of spring's pollen and rains. Hedge witches tend to their outdoor gardens in anticipation of the bountiful harvest in autumn.

As we enter the heat of summer and long days energize us, we turn our attention to the sun's effects in every area of our lives. The summer solstice is a time of heightened spiritual energy and a powerful opportunity to connect with the Divine.

For the witch, the summer solstice can be a time of personal transformation and renewal. It is a time to let go of old patterns, habits, and beliefs that no longer serve us and to embrace new beginnings and opportunities. It is also a time to connect with our inner selves and to reflect on our spiritual journey.

For witches and pagans around the globe, the summer solstice is celebrated as the festival of Litha, which is associated with fire, light, and the sun. This is a time to honor the sun god and goddess, celebrate the abundance of nature, and connect with the energies of the earth.

Some of the many deities and spirits associated with the summer solstice and this fiery time of year include:

Apollo: The Greek god of the sun, light, music, and prophecy. As the god of the sun, he is often associated with the summer solstice.

Baldur: The Norse god of light, joy, and beauty is associated with the summer solstice as a time of light and celebration.

Helios: The Greek god of the sun and solar chariot is connected to the summer solstice as a time of light and warmth.

Lugh: The Celtic god of light, skill, and mastery is recognized at the time of the summer solstice during a time of honoring abundance, harvest, and skillful craft.

Amaterasu: The Japanese Sun goddess is correlated with the summer solstice, during which time light, renewal, and growth are honored.

Hestia: The Greek goddess of the hearth and home is also one who is honored on the summer solstice as families and communities gather in joy and celebration of the longest day of the year.

Danu: The Celtic mother goddess of the earth and fertility is linked with the summer solstice as celebrants recognize it is the time of year for abundance, growth, and fertility.

The summer solstice rituals of the witch are a potent reminder to access the light within on the longest day of the year and bring forth bounty in all its forms.

FALL EQUINOX

The fall or autumnal equinox occurs on September 22 or 23, when the earth's axis is again neutral, giving us equal day and night hours.

Fall is a time of harvest, reaping, and abundant crops. We honor the Earth Mother for her bounty and nurturing in feasts at our rituals. In these rituals, we gorge on apples, root vegetables, cinnamon, hot cider, and all things autumn. Warmth fills our hearts and bellies as we prepare to settle in for the winter.

The witch's code word for the fall equinox is *balance*. With night and day exactly equal, this is the time for balance, harmony, and equalizing anything out of order or alignment. Equal parts dark and light create the perfect backdrop to:

Honor the harvest: The fall equinox is a time of harvest and abundance, and the witch honors this by celebrating the fruits of the season with feasts, offerings, and gratitude. Apple picking at orchards in upstate New York, where our parents took us each fall as a respite from city living, are etched onto my memory. The change in foliage was spectacular. Seeing ripe apples fall to the ground with a few shakes of the tree kept us in a state of wonder.

Connect with nature: As a time of transition and change, the fall equinox is the perfect opportunity for the witch to connect with nature; harvest fruit, herbs and vegetables; take long walks in the forest to observe the changing of season; and use the power of nature to bring harmony back to any aspect of self that may have been disrupted by a modern life drenched in technology and busy-ness.

Spell Work: The energy of the fall equinox is particularly potent for manifestation magick for abundance, largesse, bounty, and expansion. Because access to light and dark are perfectly equal at this time, a wide range of magickal outcomes can be spelled for, including balancing relationships, balancing the energies of the body, making homes harmonious, and any other rituals and spell work that have balance and harmony as their aim.

Offering tribute to each turn of the earth as represented by these four points is the witch's mode of acknowledging our planet and her wisdom, nurturing, and care as she orbits her life-giving sun.

THE LUNAR CYCLE

Another important cycle for the witch is the lunation cycle and its accompanying rituals. Witches have long been associated with the moon, and for good reason. The moon is cloaked in a shadowy and mysterious persona, just as is the witch. As the representation of the Goddess, the Moon is considered an active entity providing wisdom and guidance through its cycles.

The gravitational pull of the moon on earth draws all water to it, which creates the moon's effects on ocean tides and all water, including lakes, rivers, and streams. The moon even affects the water in our bodies, producing tinier high and low tides. The element of water is associated with feelings and affects mood, emotional states, and even mental faculties.

Fertility is associated with the moon, and witches who are midwives may count pregnancy according to the moon and not calendar months. When doing so, we observe that the gestation of a human baby is ten moons, or forty weeks— not nine months.

Honoring the moon and her closely associated element of water is a witch's cyclical tradition dating back to the days when witches and pagans alike openly worshiped goddesses in fields under the full moon, including these:

> **Mami Wata:** From West African mythology, this goddess is a water spirit associated with fertility, beauty, and transformation. She is often depicted holding a crescent moon and is associated with the moon's feminine energies.
>
> **Mawu Lisa:** A goddess in the religion of the Fon people of Benin, Mawu Lisa is a dual deity representing both the moon and sun. She is the female moon deity associated with creation, fertility, and change.
>
> **Ixchel:** This deity of the Mayan people of Mesoamerica is the goddess of the moon, childbirth, and weaving. She was also associated with water and fertility.
>
> **Artemis:** In Greek mythology, Artemis is the goddess of the hunt, childbirth, fertility, fecundity, and virginity. She was depicted wearing a crescent moon as a crown because of her deep association with the moon.
>
> **Hecate:** Also known as the Queen of Witches or the Goddess of the Witches, Hecate is a Greek goddess associated with the moon, witchcraft, and magic. Her legendary symbol of the torch and keys denotes her ability to light the way to hidden mysteries paired with her power to unlock their secrets for the chosen.
>
> **Luna:** Known to the ancient Romans as the Goddess of the Moon, Luna commanded a horse-drawn white chariot across the sky,

pulling the moon behind her. Luna is considered a powerful goddess in charge of ocean tides, women's menstrual cycles and fertility, and the growth of crops.

Diana: A powerful goddess associated with the moon, the hunt, wild animals of the forest, and childbirth, Diana also has a chariot, drawn by deer through the wood. She wears a crescent moon as a crown.

Chang'e: A goddess from the east in Chinese mythology who is called the Goddess of the Moon. She is depicted as a beautiful woman living on the moon with a rabbit as her familiar.

You may notice the presence of themes with the goddesses who represent the moon: fertility, menstrual cycles and childbirth, power over ocean tides and all water, and feminine energies, which are considered mysterious and dark at their heart.

The moon cycle, or the lunation cycle, refers to the changes in the moon's appearance as seen from earth while it orbits. The synodic month, or the length of time it takes the moon to orbit the earth from new moon to new moon, is 29.5 days. During this period, the moon goes through eight distinct phases, with a precursor of a dark moon. Each phase has its own energy and ritual observances.

The most widely observed of the moon cycles among witches are the new moon and full moon. Before considering each of these and their attendant ritual energies, a brief consideration of the dark moon is in order.

DARK MOON

As its name indicates, the dark moon cannot be seen from the earth at all. This is the time when the moon is positioned closest to our sun. Lasting only a few hours, the dark moon is a moment in the lunar cycle that ushers in a new moon. It has often been conflated with the new moon, although they are separate astrological events.

During the dark moon, witches prepare for the new moon and the opportunity it affords to start new endeavors. Since the dark moon lasts only a few hours, it's the perfect preparatory period before the new moon. Many witches take this time to "go dark" or to be still and abstain from magick.

NEW MOON

During a new moon, the moon is positioned between the earth and the sun. The side of the moon facing the earth is not illuminated, and only the tiniest sliver of light can be seen from earth.

The new moon provides us with the "starter" energy witches use to set new intentions, begin new projects, plant seeds, and begin cyclical ventures. This phase is a personal favorite of mine. I look forward to the new moon each month and conduct a ritual and Tarot reading for our community at this potent stage in the moon's cycle.

Since each new moon bears an astrological correspondence, it offers us guidance from the constellations on what might be appropriate ritual or spell work. A new moon in Aries is starter energy multiplied, as Aries is the first of the zodiacal procession. This new moon bodes well for rituals that include the fire energy of Aries and spell work that supports starting big projects that require a large, energetic "push."

FULL MOON

In this phase, the entire face of the moon is illuminated by the sun—to a witches' delight! The energy of the full moon is one of completion or bringing matters full circle. I call it the "cosmic take out the trash day" and I make it a point to release all patterns I am determined to end. I rid myself of these unwanted energies in the fullness of the moon, even sleeping outside under the full moon to connect more viscerally with the full moon's completion energy. I create full-moon water, which is simply fresh and pure water that is allowed to bask in the rays of the full moon for one to two nights. Full-moon water is excellent as an energetic cleanser.

This is also the perfect opportunity to give a good cleansing to crystals that are being used for altar work or ritualistic purposes. I set these crystals out overnight in the lustrous light of the full moon with a silent prayer that they be released of all old and stagnant energy they've collected on my behalf.

As is so of the new moon, each full moon bears an astrological correspondence witches use to guide rituals, divination, and spell work. A full moon in Libra could guide the witch in conducting rituals that connote air, while a full moon in Cancer would lend well to water rituals conducted at the river's edge or at the ocean. In my life as a witch, full moon energies extend to every sphere of endeavor; thus, a full moon in Libra may inspire me to finish a book I've been procrastinating on.

The complete moon cycle repeats itself every 29.5 days, bringing with it high and low tides, emotional surges and releases, and influences on all things water, to include the water in our bodies and even the amniotic sacs around the globe which incubate tomorrow's newest arrivals to the planet.

Witches, wiccans, and pagans alike honor the moon and its cycle with rituals and spell work, a nod to the ever-turning cycles of life.

Without the elements and perennial motion of the sun and moon, life on this planet would not exist. Witches are aware that our lives and the lives of all are intertwined with the elements and the solar and lunar cycles in a great cosmic web. The Earth Mother spins, rotates, and hurtles through space in an ecstatic dance with her sun and moon. We align with and attune to these heavenly bodies throughout the month as we gaze skyward morning and night, to note exactly where we are in the cycle. This is the dance of life, the cycles moving us ever onward.

WARES OF THE WITCH

———•———•———•———

T he witch practices her craft in a lair of sorts, or dedicated space, consecrated for implements, rituals, brewing concoctions, erecting altars, casting circles, and communing with spirits. All this and more takes place in my laboratorium, or magick room. Creating sacred space, or the space where magick will be practiced and implements and supplies will be stored, is an ongoing operation as the seasons change and rituals evolve along with them. Some would refer to this sacred space as a temple.

SACRED SPACE

Sacred space is created when we dispel unwanted energies and invite and fill the space with the desired energies for the magickal operation at hand. The energy of a night club, the energy of a restaurant, and the energy of a church are vastly different. The commonality is that each space was created, prepared, and energetically primed for the activities to unfold there.

The subconscious mind pays rapt attention to ritual. This is one of the reasons ritual is so moving and powerful, and why it's included in every magickal system, spiritual path, and religion on the planet. A compelling way to immediately command the attention of the subconscious mind is to transform the space around you and create a place to practice magick and perform rituals.

KITCHEN BY DAY—TEMPLE BY NIGHT

Witches work in dedicated spaces that have been energetically primed and prepared. Whether it be a kitchen counter that becomes a preparatory space for potions and tinctures, or a dedicated room with shrines and altars, sacred space, or dedicated space, is the cocoon in which we unfold powerful magick. Before beginning, cleaning and clearing is essential to rid the space of any particles or energies that are not to be included in the spell work or ritual.

CLEAN AND CLEAR

Because all energies around and in the space can leach into the magick being performed in that space, witches are keen to clean and clear the space by various means:

- Cleansing the self through sacred baths with herbs and essential oils are mainstays.
- Tending to altars and cleaning the top of the altar with fresh water, holy water, or Florida water with a clean, white cloth.
- Cleaning all implements being utilized in the ritual or magickal operation.
- Cleaning garments being worn in rituals.
- Cleaning floors of the ritual space with spiritual floor washes.

Cleansing the space raises the vibration and welcomes in spirits who are amenable to working with the witch. In addition to cleansing, clearing is performed, which includes:

- Clearing out any paraphernalia in the space that will not be used in the ritual. A witch may accumulate a plethora of magickal items over the years. Order and organization in storing these items is helpful.
- Clearing out all technology. If the sacred space is in a living room with a television, we are careful to throw a cloth over it for rituals. Televisions and anything with a black screen are portals.
- Clearing the energy. Burning sage and spraying copious amounts of Florida water are powerful energy clearing practices. Frankincense and myrrh essential oil added to water in a misting bottle makes for an excellent energy clearing spray.

When we hold our rituals in nature, less is necessary to prepare the space. Since sacred space is the home of our magickal workings, ritualistic practices as well as the place where our magickal implements are stored, it warrants utmost attention and care. Other ways to raise the vibration in your sacred space include:

Sound or Frequency: Singing bowls, bells, Native American flute, and gospel music have all been used to set the stage in sacred space and shift out of regular, waking consciousness into altered states. Higher frequencies will attune the space to the spirits we work with who will assist in the ritual or spell work.

Wind/Air Element: Opening windows and doors, especially when burning sage. Opening a door or a window as the space is being cleared allows for any untoward spirits and energies to escape.

Filling the space with light: Depending upon the spell being crafted and cast, the space will be filled with a particular color of light. In cases where the spell does not call for a particular color, filling the space with white light is advantageous. This is done in the third eye, or the imaginal realm.

Suffumigation: Certain rituals call for a specific form of suffumigation–filling the air with fumes from burning incense or other substances. Suffumigation changes the atmosphere immediately and facilitates potent results.

SYMBOLISM AND DIVINATION

Symbolism is a universal language. Spirits in other dimensions do not speak English or any other human language. Symbolism is the language used by spirits to convey messages. Though symbolism is a universal language, what each symbol means to each witch personally is not universal. What a phoenix means to me is not the same as its meaning for another witch.

Divination is seeking to know the mind of the Divine. It is the witch's practice of seeking knowledge or insight through the interpretation of omens, signs, symbols, and other means that have spiritual or magickal significance. Divination is the art of accessing information that is not available through ordinary senses or logical reasoning. Tools of divination include Tarot cards, tea leaves, coffee grinds, bones, cowrie shells, runes, and pendulums. Over the eons, witches have used a plethora of devices for divination, which reveals an important truth: the device does not matter as much as the witch's intuition and reception of information from beyond this world.

Witches use divination as part of our spiritual practices. Divination helps us to determine the best tools for the job; understand hidden influences that may be affecting the outcome of spell work; consider the cosmos and the astrological influences present; and make decisions about seemingly mundane matters such as cars, homes, and careers by seeing these as matters of spirituality and ascension.

The wares and tools of the witch are many, and each has an important role in bringing about the outcomes being conjured.

TAROT

Tarot is one of the most potent spiritual tools we have as a human race, and it no longer resides exclusively in the domain of the witch. Witches work with Tarot to build up a symbolic dictionary in consciousness. This symbolism is critical for divination and dream interpretation. We can also interpret the messages of symbolism for real-world use.

The origins of this divination tool are nebulous. The book of Tarot consists of seventy-eight cards belonging to two divisions called the Major Arcana, consisting of the first twenty-two cards (numbered 0 to 21) and the Minor Arcana, consisting of fifty-six cards arranged in four suits of twelve cards each. The suits of pentacles, swords, wands, and cups correspond to the elements of earth, air, fire, and water, respectively. The four aces of the Tarot deck make for excellent symbols on an altar or in rituals for the element they each represent.

Tarot, a pictorial representation of the journey of the soul, is a powerful spiritual tool for the witch and figures prominently in our arsenal. Tarot can be used for meditation on mysteries, as it invokes unconscious energies deep within the psyche.

These cards can also be used for understanding the hidden elements within a certain situation that might not be readily apparent on the third-dimensional plane of consciousness. When one does a reading and sees the Moon card appear, for instance, it can be a warning that there are hidden elements at work that will affect the outcome of the ritual or spell. It is important to seek wisdom from planes beyond the conscious mind to reveal these hidden elements to the individual.

Tarot can be used for alignment with cycles of the moon as witches engage new moon and full moon readings in a ritualistic observance and acknowledgment of the celestial orb's effects on our psyche and outcomes. Tarot readings can also reveal past influences affecting the present or the future, as well as present potentialities and possible future outcomes. While no Tarot reading can determine the future with certainty, it can show potentialities and probable outcomes if the querent continues the path chosen. This gives us an opportunity to exercise the power of choice. We are always free to choose to change our direction, once we see where it will lead, or to continue the path we are pursuing, if it is to our liking.

The past, present, and future potentialities within the book of Tarot align with the witches' threefold take on reality: past, present, and future; maiden, mother, and crone; and the symbol of the three phases of the moon: waxing, full, and waning, as pictured on the crown of The High Priestess, the archetype symbolized on Tarot card #2.

Tarot is also a potent power for accessing the Divine. My first Tarot teacher, many years ago, referred to the first twenty-two cards as "keys" because they unlock dimensions of consciousness through meditation and reflection.

We begin, with the Tarot deck, to immerse ourselves in a book of symbolism. To effectively perform magick and commune with spirits in different dimensions, we must learn the language of symbolism. Tarot enables and speeds this process. It also can be used for meditation, reflection, journal prompts, storytelling, divination, contemplation, and more. There is no limit to what Tarot can do once engaged and consulted.

When I was in the early stages of learning Tarot, more than eighteen years ago, my Tarot teacher recommended that we work with one card at a time, over the period of a week, even sleeping with that card under the pillow. This full immersion in one card at a time proved priceless. It was like living with a Tarot mentor each week. The dreams I had were bizarre, yet I learned so much from the experience that it was worthwhile.

Over the years, Tarot deck upon Tarot deck has made its way to me. Many have come so that I could pass them on to a Tarot beginner or to another magickal friend. This is the way of Tarot. If the true owner of the deck is not likely to go into a magick shop and buy that deck, the deck will still make its way to the true owner by way of people who are already working with Tarot.

Witches have found that the best way to learn Tarot is to read the cards daily. Tarot books and Tarot teachers are amazing—I've had my share of both—yet none of these will rival what can be learned through a dedicated practice of experientially engaging and reading Tarot, and then carefully noting all results in a grimoire. Tarot is a teacher extraordinaire.

PENDULUMS

A pendulum is a weighted object, many times a crystal, attached to a chain or string. Pendulums can be used to gain insight and clarity on issues, questions, or situations.

Pendulum *dowsing*, also known as *divining*, is a technique used to receive guidance, insights, or answers to yes or no questions. The pendulum is held steady and asked a question, and the answer is determined by the way that the pendulum swings. The pendulum must be attuned so the witch can determine which direction indicates a *yes* and which direction indicates a *no* answer. Some pendulums swing back and forth for *no*, and side to side for *yes*. Others swing clockwise or counterclockwise. The direction is easily discernible by asking the pendulum to show a *yes* answer and then asking it to show a *no* answer.

Pendulums can also be used for healing and balancing the body's energy, as well as for detecting imbalances or blockages in the body's energy system. Witches who are healers and medical intuitives can use pendulums for just this purpose.

The use of a pendulum is based on the principle of dowsing, which is the practice of using a tool, such as a pendulum or a divining rod, to detect hidden objects or information. The practice of dowsing has been used for centuries in various cultures and traditions and is still in use around the world. The pendulum is popular, easy to use, and reliably accurate when mastered.

MAGICK WANDS

The history of the magick wand can be traced back to ancient times, where it was used as a tool for both practical and spiritual purposes. As far back as ancient Egypt, wands were used as symbols of power and authority. They were depicted in hieroglyphics as a symbol of the gods. Wands were also used in magickal rites such as healing, divination, and protection.

In ancient Greece and Rome, wands were part of the practice of magick, particularly in the form of wand-waving or casting spells. Philosophers and teachers also used wands to point out important ideas or concepts, much as modern-day teachers have been known to use pointers or lasers.

In medieval Europe, magicians and alchemists believed that the wand could be utilized to channel and direct energy. They used wands in ceremonial and ritualistic practices such as blessing objects or consecrating sacred spaces.

The modern witch can still use a wand as a tool for directing and focusing energy, as well as for spell casting and rituals.

I have several magick wands that are used for focusing the energy to cast a circle, perform a spell, contact spirits, and help with a variety of other magickal and mundane purposes.

Different types of wood used for creating and carving magick wands are associated with specific magickal properties and symbolic meanings:

> **Ash**—healing, protection, spiritual journeys, and the element of water. It carries the power to purify and cleanse.
>
> **Oak**—strength, power, endurance, and the element of fire. Oak has the power to enhance creativity and manifestation.

Willow—intuition, dreams, emotions, and the element of water. It has the power to enhance psychic abilities and divination.

Elder—protection, healing, wisdom, and the element of earth. It has the power to bring good fortune and prosperity.

Holly—protection, strength, transformation, and the element of fire. It has the power to banish negativity and promote growth and change.

Birch—new beginnings, purification, and renewal as well as the element of air. It has the power to enhance communication and clarity of thought.

The perfect wand will always make its way to the witch when the time is right and the witch is ready.

CRYSTALS

The witch knows the importance of connecting with the natural world, and crystals are a means to do so. Crystals are part of the earth element and they possess energetic and healing properties. Witches might use these important materials for:

Energy amplification—to amplify and direct energy, which is used for magickal purposes to include spell crafting and casting, manifestation, and healing.

Healing—enhancing the ability to balance chakras, soothe anxiety, or promote emotional healing.

Divination—crystal gazing or scrying, where the crystal becomes a tool to access intuitive awareness and insights.

Protection—to create talismans or amulets for physical or spiritual safety.

Connection to nature—to tap into the energies and vibrations of the earth element.

CAULDRONS

Cauldrons are often associated with witches and magick. They have been used for centuries in various cultures and traditions around the world for:

Mixing and brewing potions: Combining and brewing various herbs, oils, and other ingredients to create healing, magickal, or ceremonial potions.

Scrying: Gazing into a reflective surface to receive insights, visions, or messages. A cauldron filled with water can be used as a scrying tool, as the water can reflect images or symbols that hold meaning.

Burning incense: Holding incense or smudge sticks, which can be used to cleanse or purify a space or to create a certain atmosphere for ritual or meditation.

Holding offerings: Carrying offerings or sacrifices during rituals or ceremonies.

Cooking: Performing practical functions, such as cooking over a fire or carrying hot coals.

A dear friend who is a magickal practitioner has more than thirty cauldrons that he uses for everything from making candles to cooking to brewing apple cider. A cauldron is a multi-use device for witches.

SIGILS

During a dark period in my life, I realized I was having more trouble than necessary in relationships and my life due to issues I could trace back to early childhood. Through meditation and ritualistic practice, I discovered my problems were about trust. My trust issues had been a negative current running through my life, leaving damage in its wake.

My solution was a *sigil*—a potent, hand-drawn symbol infused with intention. My sigil was ignited, activated, and filled with the energy of trust. I drew the sigil repeatedly, each time rooting into trust until I could feel the energetic foundation under me was rock solid. Later, I had the words Faith and Trust tattooed on my right and left feet, respectively.

A sigil is a symbol or design created with the intention of representing a specific goal, desire, or intention. Sigils are used in magickal practices, particularly in chaos magick, as a way of focusing the practitioner's will and subconscious mind on a particular outcome.

The creation of a sigil can involve writing out words that form the essence of the desired result, then removing all vowels in the words. The remaining letters are then combined and manipulated to create a unique symbol or sigil. Sigils can also be created by using numbers or Hebrew letters for their potency.

Once a sigil is created, it's charged with energy through meditation and used as a point of focus for the witch's intention and will. Some practitioners may use sigils in rituals or spellwork, while others might carry them on their person as a talisman or use them in visualization exercises. Some put sigils away after their creation, so that the practitioner can "forget" about the working, so as not to become attached to outcomes or lust for a result, rather than letting it unfold in the natural order.

The witch will use sigils in a multitude of ways:

Spellwork: Witches incorporate sigils to focus intention and energy on a specific goal or outcome. The sigil may be included in spell casting; used to charge a talisman or amulet; or incorporated into a ritual. After the magickal operation with the sigil is done, it is put away. Removing the sigil from sight is a way of releasing the result, rather than being fixated on it. Many times, I've come across an old sigil under a candle holder or in a book while rearranging my sacred space and have smiled, knowing that the outcome was received.

Divination: Witches use sigils in divination practices, including scrying in a black mirror or any reflective surface; as part of Tarot readings; and in reading tea leaves. The sigil focuses the divination tool and may be incorporated into the meaning of the reading.

Protection: Sigils can protect us and others. A sigil charged with protective energy may be carried or worn as an amulet.

Manifestation: Witches can use sigils in manifestation practices including visualizations and affirmations, to focus intention on a specific, tangible outcome or a desired experience.

Sigils are powerful tools for witches to connect with the subconscious mind and create dramatic changes, as I did with my trust sigil.

Some witches also use sigils as a "calling card" to represent a specific entity one desires to summon. The magick of sigils and symbols is that they encapsulate and express a thousand or more thoughts or ideas in one tiny set of dots and lines. This makes them a type of magickal shorthand that takes giant outcomes and puts them into one tiny, pulsing energy symbol that becomes a magnetic beacon to one's desires.

CANDLE MAGICK AND RITUALS

A recent class I taught included a candle-burning ritual for more than eighty people. Even as an experienced witch, I'd never burned that many candles at one time, so it was a new venture for all of us. When all the candles were lit, the energy in the room was palpable. The students reported their substantial results. I slept that night in my sacred space, arising occasionally to tend the candles, read their waxy appearances, and take notes in a grimoire.

The magick of candles is that like many divinatory tools, they tell a story.

THE HISTORY OF CANDLE-BURNING

The exact origin of the practice is not known, but it's believed that witches have used candles for more than 5,000 years. The ancient Egyptians used candles—theirs were reeds soaked in animal fat—as early as 3000 B.C. They placed candles in tombs near the mummified body, hoping to provide warmth for the deceased and to light their path to the afterlife. Witches today burn white candles for those who have recently transitioned for this purpose.

Egyptians also used candles in their temples to honor the gods and goddesses, placing them in front of statues of the gods as an offering. The candlelight was believed to symbolize the presence of the Divine, and the flickering flame was seen as a representation of the eternal cycle of life and death.

Candles played an important role in ancient Egyptian spiritual practices, used for a variety of purposes related to their beliefs about the afterlife and the Divine. In the same way, candles play an important role for witches and spiritual practitioners today.

CANDLE MAGICK FOR BIRTHDAY CELEBRATIONS

Egyptians were also the first on record to recognize birthdays—but only for their pharaohs. They celebrated each anniversary of the pharaoh's coronation, which was considered his "birth" as a god.

We know the Egyptians also used candles. But it was another culture that put them on cakes.

The Greeks stuck candles into moon-shaped cakes and offered them to the goddess Artemis—ruler of the moon and the hunt—on the sixth day of each lunar month. The lit candles represented the glow of the moon, and smoke from the candles was thought to carry prayers and wishes to heaven.

Elements of these two practices became a modern candle ritual most of us have participated in: candles on top of birthday cakes. We build on practices from our forebears. Candle magick is one of the powerful practices we inherited.

MULTIDIMENSIONAL NATURE OF CANDLES

Candles work magick on multiple dimensions at the same time.

When someone transitions out of this life, it is not unusual to burn a white candle for them. The effects would be felt on this plane and also experienced on other planes of existence, providing more white light for the soul as it ascends.

This is one of the many ways candles help us deal with life and death.

Witches are instinctively and intuitively drawn to candles, even if we don't know why. Before I began intentionally practicing magick, and long before I knew of any occult meaning, my home was full of candles. I was unconsciously working candle magick.

CANDLE MAGICK APPLICATIONS

What do witches know about candles?

- Candlelight represents lunar, solar, and Divine energy.
- The smoke of the extinguished candle can be used to carry prayers and intentions heavenward.
- Witches read how fast the candle burns, how much the flame dances, what traces of wax are left on the sides of the glass container, the color of the smoke, and more for messages about the subject of candle magick.
- Dressing a candle—adding essential oils, anointing oils, and herbs to our candles—magnifies the intention's power exponentially.
- Candles may encourage spirit visitations and other supernatural occurrences.
- Candle colors can represent and honor the energy of the elements in a sacred space.

CANDLE COLOR CORRESPONDENCES

Candle colors speak to us intuitively. Specific candle colors have traditionally been used for certain purposes. Here are a few color correspondences to keep in mind if choosing to light a candle for magickal or spiritual purposes:

White: An appropriate color for all things spiritual. Good for light, purity, and unveiling shadow energies. Also used for helping loved ones who've crossed over to ascend.

Red: Passion, fire, flames, movement, action, and spiritual self. The element of fire. The Wands suit in Tarot.

Blue: Calming, cleansing, restorative, flowing, emotional self. The element of water. The Cups suit in Tarot.

Pink: Heart, love, friendship, healing, hope, inspiration.

Green: Abundance, creativity (especially for authors and other creatives), healing, nature, wellness, wholeness, freshness, new birth, physical self. The element of earth. The Pentacles suit in Tarot.

Yellow: Earthy, grounding, solidifying, mental self. The element of air. The Swords suit in Tarot.

Purple/Violet: Royalty, ascension, crown chakra, divinity, spirit communication.

Orange: Sensuality, sexuality, energizing, expansive.

Black: Cloaking, subduing, destroying, halting, hiding, reversing, containing, constricting.

VESTMENTS, CLOAKS, AND ROBES

Superheroes wear capes and witches wear cloaks. Our wardrobe can transform us. As the superhero changes from an ordinary person into a legend, their new persona warrants a wardrobe change. This helps shift the superhero's psyche and self-concept; in some cases, even their speech transforms. They become a new, super powerful entity.

We've all experienced the change in a person's demeanor and bearing when they don ceremonial attire. A judge wears a black gown we respect. A nun wears a habit we recognize and honor. A priest is immediately known by his garb, as is a shaman or a monk.

The witch, too, dons magickal garb, robes, and vestments to take on a different persona appropriate for the working or ritual at hand and to instantly create the dramatic shift in consciousness required to practice powerful magick. When a whole *coven* or group of witches who are all similarly clad are practicing together, the experience is otherworldly.

I remember the first magickal cloak I purchased for myself after coming to the realization that I was a witch and that the powerful being inside me deserved regard and expression. It was a floor-length purple cloak with a hood.

The first ritual for which I wore the cloak was a Samhain fire festival I attended several years ago at the home of a Druid. He lived in a house set in the middle of vast acreage on which he had created an outdoor temple in the woods. The Druid conducted the ritual with three witches each year on Samhain, just as his ancestor had carefully prescribed. I attended and participated in several of these potent rituals, with life-transforming results.

Because all the participants were cloaked or wore magickal vestments, the occasion took on an air of magick that was palpable. Donning my cloak before setting off into the woods with a clan of magickal beings, led by a Druid, set the stage—in dramatic fashion, I might add—to shift my mind out of waking consciousness and into an altered state.

This is how witches become superheroes.

As a practicing witch, having one's lair and wares in order is essential to spiritual growth and attainment, performing effective rituals, crafting and casting spells for Divine outcomes, and remaining in rich commune with helpful spirits. A witch is no different in this regard from any practitioner one would seek for help, such as a doctor or midwife. Healing practitioners operate in a space conducive to successful outcomes.

Now that our sacred space and implements are ready, let's continue to the rituals.

THE WITCH'S GATEWAY
TO WORLDS BEYOND

*I*t is late at night on a crisp evening in December on the red rocks of Sedona, Arizona. Our coven of witches traverses the rocks on a slim and dusty trail with one intention: to honor the winter solstice.

The rocks and cold earth crunch under our feet as we make our way up a trail most humans would not tread at this time of night. The witches feel the ancient impulse of nature. Darkness has descended and we are celebrating that there is no light, knowing it will return. While swathed in darkness, we find ourselves at home. As we climb the trail, we become aware of movement in the underbrush a short distance off. A family of wild javelinas scavenging for cacti and other delicacies scurries off in another direction. We smile in silent acknowledgment that the night creatures, like us, are also stirring.

The crisp air nips our skin and our warm breath leaves our bodies in puffs of mist. We are warmly clad for the night ahead, which promises to be a long one as we honor what would appear to be the disappearance of the sun for three days before it is born anew. We are armed with incense, candles, crystals, altar cloths, our fire-making utensils, a vessel for the fire, ancestor money, and the intention and will to align with the great seasons and cycles of the cosmos and to remember we are one with it all. We know that in our alignment with the seasons and cycles of the sun, moon, nature, and even life and death itself, we develop deep symbiosis with all that is. This alignment affords us access to unfathomable power.

The ancestor money we've bought with us is to connect with those who have gone before us. Some of our ancestors crossed the great ocean from the west and south of Africa to the Caribbean and the southern harbors of America. Others of our ancestors hailed from Europe: the Scottish, Celtic, and British. Still others are descended from ancestors from other places around the globe. No matter where we have come from, we agree on this chilly night that we are here to honor the season of winter. We willingly enter the depths of the winter to rest, renew, and incubate new life that will not become visible until the spring.

We find our holy lair in nature on a rocky clearing high up the trail, where we have held rituals for many years in the dark of night. Here in our outdoor temple, we gaze upon the moon undisturbed, commune with nature, and crush fresh juniper berries between our fingers, inhaling their heady fragrance. Here, it is only us and the elements. We feel sublimely at home.

We set our sacred space, build a fire, assemble ourselves, and begin our ritual with deep breathing and prayer. We invoke our spirit guides, angels, enlightened ancestors, and the helpers who reside beyond the veil. Then we begin. The air has been impregnated with energy and infused with magick. We know we are at our purest and most open to the energies present.

In the fire, we burn ancestor money to strengthen the unbreakable bonds with our lineage, so that wisdom flows in an unbroken line to us in all we undertake. We know we do not have to repeat the mistakes or failures of the past. We gain access to the wisdom, knowledge, and power of our ancestors as we speak their names and uplift their spirits with our remembrance and acknowledgment. We are in forever union with those who have gone before us.

As witches, we honor the cycle of life and death as an unbroken circle. We stand as doulas for birth, death, and every station in between. Our ancestors had to release a human shell to travel to the great beyond, and so our veneration of those who have crossed to the other side serves as a tribute to death as the natural ending of one way of existence and birth into another.

This ritual on the red rocks of Sedona on a cold night with a coven of witches who are intentional about alignment with nature, life, and death—and all its seasons and cycles—is an ode to the life of the witch.

It is a life of ritual and observance, of celebration and festivals, of magick and the craft, all illumined and electrified through our intention, will, and unbreakable interdependence with all that is.

RITUALS

The definition of the word ritual is:

> "A religious or solemn ceremony consisting of a series of actions performed according to a prescribed order."
>
> or
>
> "The established form for a ceremony, specifically: the order of words prescribed for a religious ceremony."
>
> or
>
> "Ritual observance, specifically: a system of rites; a ceremonial act or action; an act or series of acts regularly repeated in a set precise manner."

Though there are many types of rituals, in this context we are referring to an act or set of actions, undertaken in a focused and intentional manner and infused with symbolic meaning that have as an intention to acknowledge and put us squarely in touch with the energies present within and all around us.

Ritual is sacred. It connects us with the Divine and is a portal to the otherworldly.

One of the other most potent aspects of ritual is memorability. We do not forget deeply meaningful rituals performed in a sacred and devout manner. They are etched in consciousness, thus forming a perfect pathway for the manifestation of desires. This pathway is an energetic river upon which our desires can be continually conveyed to us.

CONDUCTING MAGICKAL RITUALS

A potent aspect of our rituals is to disconnect from the ordinary and enter altered states of consciousness where spirit communion and other consciousness-expanding experiences can be induced. The witch engages in specific steps before, during, and after spellwork or other spiritual work, such as a sacred bath, lighting candles, and casting a circle, etc.

Rituals may include:

> **Tarot reading:** The witch creates sacred space in her temple, casts a circle, and engages in a full Tarot reading. She then records the reading in detail, including drawing pictures of each card, in a Tarot grimoire. I practiced this ritual for each full moon for more than a year. The growth and guidance I garnered were indispensable.

> **Daily morning or evening spiritual practices:** These may involve ritual bathing; entering sacred space to light incense and candles; meditation; journaling; breathwork; and tending to one's altar. Morning spiritual practices are engaged during the "witching hour" of three a.m. to six a.m.

These practices elicit expanded states of awareness. Rituals alter our consciousness. Long after rituals have been completed and the utensils have been put away, the experience lingers in memory.

ALTERING CONSCIOUSNESS

How do rituals alter our consciousness? They work in many ways.

First, they are undertaken at unusual times, in non-normal locations, wearing ritual clothing, and usually performed as an act or set of actions that include speaking unusual words and incantations. Rituals rip us away from our third-dimensional, usual states of being and casts us into the liminal. Rituals aid us in remembering we are far beyond human. They afford us a means to access latent energies within that enable us to perform greater works of magick and witchcraft.

Because rituals are emblazoned on our consciousness, they are remembered. When we reflect on any specific ritual, if we become still and tune into the frequencies present when we performed the ritual, we can remember its details and feel its effects.

The evocative power of ritual is without parallel, which is why it has been sought and practiced by humans over eons. We mark important occasions with rituals. Weddings as joyous celebrations of love include important rituals designed to remind the couple of their vows of union, as well as elicit the support and love of the community around that couple to help them keep their vows of love to each other. The wedding is one of the most potent rituals we have.

We engage in rituals for our loved ones who have passed on, to remind us that by acknowledging death, we remember to live. Rituals are engaged for childbirth, rites of passage when crossing from one stage of life to another, and for all we deem important.

The witch is called upon and may officiate many of these rituals, as they represent the cycles and seasons of our lives that parallel the cycles and seasons of nature and the entire cosmos we inhabit.

LIGHT AND SHADOW

In psychology, the concept of the "shadow" refers to the unconscious aspects of the psyche that we often repress or deny. The shadow is comprised of thoughts, feelings, and impulses that are considered unacceptable, undesirable, or even shameful. These can include aspects of ourselves that we don't want to acknowledge, such as negative traits, fears, or desires.

If we do not address these denied aspects of self, they control us. When we recognize and acknowledge the shadow, we achieve the aims of individuation, which makes us whole to experience a fulfilling life.

The witch engages in shadow work to become a more potent healer and practitioner. Witches can take on this work courageously, since we have never been afraid of the dark. We relish it, revel in it, and seek it. We know the dark holds secrets and power.

When the shadow is addressed, a tremendous amount of creative energy is made available.

Every villain we perceive as scary or menacing is a representation of the shadow self as it seeks to be recognized, accepted, and integrated. How powerful we become when we clearly see all our inner villains, accept them, and make peace with them!

We plumb the depths of our consciousness in this ritual to facilitate individuation.

THE RITUAL OF LIGHT AND SHADOW

In this ritual, you'll create two lists and expound on each item.

The first list will contain your "light" qualities: what you love about yourself, your gifts, your talents, your Divine attributes, and any and all "good" qualities you can call to mind that apply to you.

The second will be a list of your "dark" aspects: what you don't love about yourself, what you see in yourself as dangerous or foreign, what you project onto others, what you try to keep hidden, and what you believe to be "bad" about yourself.

PURPOSE OF THE RITUAL

Before beginning, we must be clear about our purpose so that we can craft a powerful intention. This ritual is for:

Self-awareness: Becoming aware of all the shadow energies that reside in consciousness. Awareness is 80 percent of transformation. We cannot change what we refuse to see.

Sovereign power: The more we know ourselves, the more empowered we become. As witches, we own our powerful nature. Great magick cannot be wrought without a visceral connection to power.

Peace: With greater self-awareness comes peace.

Transformation: It isn't necessary for every shadow aspect to leave. The purpose is to become aware of the shadow self and integrate this energy for maximum creative power. Transformation will naturally occur as we choose to tend to our consciousness and perform deep shadow work.

PREPARATION FOR THE RITUAL

This ritual can be performed as often as desired or required. Once will not do the job. Make exploring yourself habitual. You might want to conduct this ritual on each full moon for a year. Allow two to three hours for this ritual, not including your ritual bath. As always, when engaging in rituals or spiritual processes, prepare:

- Yourself: Spiritually, mentally, emotionally, physically.

- Your environment: Set a sacred space as you normally would. Select a location for the ritual where you will not be disturbed. Nature is best, or in your sacred space in your home.

- Spirit allies: Invite your spirit team of angels, spirit guides, enlightened ancestors, ascended masters, animal totems, and those beings you work with in spirit realms.

- Your materials: To access the deepest parts of you.

- Your tools: Magickal implements to facilitate the ritual at hand.

MATERIALS AND TOOLS

- Two new grimoires or magickal journals: One will serve as the book of light and the other as the book of shadow. When selecting grimoires, be sure color, size, and style are sympathetic to the work you're doing.

- Five candles: One for each of the four elements, plus a white candle for Higher Self. The elemental candles will be red for fire, green for earth, blue for water, and yellow for air. You can also use whatever colors work best for you. The white candle should be placed in the center. You may "dress" the candles if desired, though it's not required.

- Altar: You'll construct an altar especially for this purpose.

- Water: A clear vessel—I use a glass or a vase—filled with fresh, pure water all the way to the top, such that a bubble appears at the top of the vessel.

- Fire: A fire pit is useful if you have access to one. Otherwise, the candles will serve as representatives of the element of fire.

- Air: Incense scented with nag champa for general spiritual work, Indian temple incense, or any incense conducive to the working.

- Flowers: Red roses are perfect for this kind of work, because they speak of love and this is a self-love ritual of sorts. Also good are any white flowers, for the light self, and deeper-hued flowers for the shadow self.

- Three large crystals: Selenite and clear quartz are perfect for this kind of work and for any work where the desire is to see clearly and to pierce the veil. Purple amethyst for the crown chakra and contact with spirit beings can be used. Pink quartz is also appropriate for this ritual as it reflects the pure unconditional love of the heart. Make sure one of the three crystals is black—such as black obsidian or onyx—for the shadow self.

- Tarot cards: The High Priestess (Key #2), The Sun (Key #19) or The Star (Key #17), and The Devil (Key #15). The High Priestess grants access into realms of the unconscious. The Sun or The Star (whichever you choose to use, based on intuition) represents the light. The Devil represents the shadow aspects of self. Bring to the ritual any other Tarot cards you're inspired to include.

- Essential oils and/or herbs: Davana, rose, melissa, geranium, and ylang ylang essential oils. These are selected for their flowery and calming nature. Consciousness is ever unfolding, like a flower. The flowering of consciousness is represented by the flowery aromas. Herbs can be used here as well, especially herbs used in spirituality and for opening the third eye such as holy basil, star anise, gotu kola, sage, or hibiscus. Use herbs and essential oils you're intuitively led to integrate into this working.

- Consecrated anointing oil: An oil such as olive oil or another natural oil that has been infused with frankincense and myrrh essential oils.

- Pennies: In this ritual, a circle will be cast with pennies.

- A beautiful purple pen: For writing in a high-vibration color. You might want to craft a special pen for your workings.

- A wand or dagger: Used for casting the circle and establishing a prescribed perimeter of protection and designated area for the spiritual energy raised during this ritual.

- White clothing: If desired, to lovingly bring all aspects of self to the light, wear white. We're revealing what's hidden in the unconscious so that we become aware, assume innate power, and become master of self. If white doesn't work for you, feel free to use any color that represents the work at hand. Being nude, or "skyclad" as witches would call it, is also a perfect option for this ritual, as we're bringing everything hidden to the light.

STEPS FOR THE RITUAL

Be sure all items are cleansed, cleared, and blessed for the ritual. When conducting the ritual, trust your intuition and make any necessary adjustments, always implicitly following your Divine revelation.

1. Ritual Bath

Take a ritual bath with the above-mentioned essential oils and/or herbs. Cleansing one's body and aura are an important start to this ritual. After exiting the bath, dry off and anoint your head, hands, feet, and heart with consecrated anointing oil. Then don your magickal undergarments (if desired) and white robes or go nude.

2.   Write Your Intention Statement

You will write your intention so that it can be stated in the ritual. Here's a sample intention statement for this working:

> "It is my intention to experience peace and power as I lovingly explore my consciousness to uncover any shadow aspects of self that I may currently be unaware of, and that have been causing untoward effects/events in my life. I am ruthlessly committed to a life of power and self-mastery. I now engage this ritual knowing the results are perfectly returned to me, in perfect timing, by the unfailing love and law of this universe. So mote it be!"

3.   Construct the Altar

Set up your altar, which will be in front of you to the north, outside of the magick circle. Arrange it beautifully. Take your time. Add to your altar:

- The clear vessel you've chosen, filled with fresh, pure water in the manner described.
- The incense, lighted, so that the smell wafts through the air, preparing the space for deep spiritual work.
- The fresh flowers in a beautiful vase of water.
- The crystals. Place one each in front of the water, incense, and flowers.

4.   Cast the Circle

You'll now create a circle of pennies on the floor or the ground, depending upon where you choose to perform this ritual. The purpose is to clearly outline the protected space. Create the circle to be nine feet in diameter.

Before creating the penny circle, place the following items in the center so you have access to them once the circle is cast:

- Your two grimoires. Place the book of light on your right, with the Sun or the Star Tarot card atop it to fill it with light. Place the book of shadow on the left with The Devil card atop it to reveal the shadow. Place the High Priestess card in the center of the two books. She will grant you access to the deep well of the unconscious.
- The five candles. Place each colored candle in the appropriate direction (east, south, west, and north) and place the white candle in the center, where you'll be sitting.
- A wand or dagger.
- Matches or another fire source.

Be sure that you have everything you require with you inside the circle. Once the ritual has begun, there is no exiting the circle until it is complete.

After you have gathered all the items you will need, place the pennies in a circle around you and your magick items.

5. Spirit Invocation

Stand in the center of your penny circle. Raise your attention, arms, and hands heavenward. Call in the spirits you are connected to with the following invocations. Speak the invocations with vigor and power in your voice. Speak the invocations over and over until you sense the presence of the spirits. Your entire being must be viscerally engaged in invoking these spirits.

> To invoke the higher self: Look upward and say,
> "Higher self, I ask for your loving presence as I dive into the depths of my deepest, darkest interior so that I may know myself. I desire to know and understand all aspects of my being and to integrate these into a tapestry that is a perfect mirror and reflection of my Divine self."

As you acknowledge the presence of higher self, light the white candle. Then light each of the elemental candles in this order: water, fire, earth, and air.

> To invoke the enlightened ancestors: Look at your heart and say,
>
> "To the enlightened ancestors who attend me, including (name your matrilineal and patrilineal ancestral line as far back as you know it), I ask for your power and presence to be with me now. I humbly ask for your wisdom and guidance to attend me in all my affairs and in this undertaking so that I may fulfill the expression of my Divine potential and achieve individuation."
>
> To invoke the animal totems: Say,
>
> "To the power animals who guide and protect me in this incarnation, I call upon you for your strength, wisdom, and power now, for this undertaking of self-gnosis."
>
> To invoke the Christ: Say,
>
> "Ascended master and wayshower Christ, I beseech your presence here, knowing you are the keeper of the Age of Pisces and a great mystic. I ask that you attend me as I do what you did when, after forty days and forty nights of fasting, you conquered your shadow self. I seek to meet and overcome the three great temptations of my shadow self, so that I may rise above pride or hubris and lust for fame; lack and all symptoms of limitation in my consciousness; and the doubt that would tempt me to deny my true Divine self."

6. Cast the Circle

After invoking the spirits, face the east, the land of the rising sun and spiritual enlightenment, holding your wand or dagger in both hands and pointed away from you.

Cast the circle by drawing the circle with the dagger in the air around yourself moving clockwise. As you cast the circle, see a wall of light around you from the floor to the heavens. Continue all the way around to complete the circle. When complete, you are surrounded with a wall of celestial light. Know you are protected, guarded, and guided, both physically and spiritually.

7. Meditate

Be seated in the center of the circle in a meditative state for twenty minutes or longer. When you've relaxed into an altered state of consciousness, proceed to the next step.

8. Write

You'll start with your book of light. Write all the qualities about yourself that you love. Write your strengths, gifts, talents, skills, and your greatest accomplishments. Write your big wins and everything about yourself that makes you proud to be you.

Take all the time you need to fully write out everything you love about yourself and why. This is a love letter to yourself. Smile. Breathe and be thorough.

Next, bring forth your book of shadow and write out all you secretly hate or do not like about yourself, and dare not entertain, even in your deepest, darkest thoughts. Write out the things that make you angry and why. Write out all the aspects of self you wish you could change, as these represent hidden shards of self-hatred. Write out all the mistakes you've made, and how your mistakes and choices created less than ideal situations in your life. Write out all that grates on your nerves about you and your life as it currently is. Write out what irritates you about other people, recognizing these as projections of undesirable or unknown aspects of self.

In both grimoires, write freely as the stream of consciousness flows through your mind, with no editing. You may be surprised at what comes out on paper. Whatever it is, bless it, forgive it, and keep going.

9. Pause

After you've recorded your thoughts in both books:

- Pause. Be still.
- Breathe. Take ten long, slow, deep breaths.
- Still your mind. Your head may be swirling a bit.
- Give thanks for your insights.

Allow anything else to come to you that you might have missed. Add these as they come up. When complete, repeat, beginning with the pause.

Be patient with yourself. Love yourself through the ritual, knowing that the process may not be sweet, but the results will be.

10. Completion

When you feel complete, take these steps:

- Fan the feeling of gratitude within yourself.
- Stand and stretch to allow yourself to return to full, waking consciousness. Move slowly.
- When you're ready, pick up your wand or dagger and open the circle by pointing east and moving around the circle counterclockwise to release the white wall of light.
- Snuff each of the five candles in the reverse order they were lit.

- Remove the pennies in the opposite order in which you laid them down and place them in a penny receptacle for another ritual.
- Remove all items from the area you were working in.

WHAT TO DO WITH THE INFORMATION

You may have received visions, insights, and revelations about exactly how your shadow has been working against you. What are we to do with all this information?

Nothing yet. We cannot assume that there's always something to do after discovering deep, dark, hidden aspects of self that are undesirable. You will receive the next steps from the Divine, along with answers and supernatural support. Healing modalities will flow to you that you'll recognize as appropriate for you at this stage of healing. It might be plant medicine, acupuncture, books, or other healing modalities that will present themselves to you to address everything that was uncovered in consciousness and to correct it all.

As you may intuit, this is an ongoing exercise. Once is not sufficient to address all the shadow aspects we deny. Allow your intuition to guide you on how often to engage this ritual.

RITUAL FOR LEAPING INTO A NEW SPIRITUAL IDENTITY

This ritual is specifically designed for shedding the old and taking on a new spiritual identity in a dramatic leap over a besom. It is leaving the old self behind and being born anew as an elevated Divine being. Perform this ritual when:

- You become aware you are repeating old patterns of thinking and feeling and are ready to eliminate these and ascend.

- You see yourself recycling old beliefs from parents, society, religion, and any other outside influence and are experiencing the negative effects of these worn-out belief structures.
- You are aware of the presence of wounds and past hurts that are blocking, inhibiting, or in any way impeding your experience of bliss right here and now, with yourself and in your relationships.
- You are moving to a new home.
- You are leaving an old job.
- You require a fresh start.

MATERIALS AND TOOLS

- Meditative music
- A besom
- Rose petals, which can be procured or can be dried from fresh roses you've saved
- An altar space covered with a white cloth. It can be a small table.
- A clear glass bowl
- Holy water, which can be procured from a Catholic church or you can make your own by praying over the water
- One white candle
- Eucalyptus essential oil
- Nag champa or frankincense incense
- Sage or smudge stick
- Fresh white flowers—geraniums are ideal—either potted or in a vase with water
- Salt —table salt or sea salt are perfect
- Florida water
- A white towel
- White attire. This can be as simple as a dress or shirt—or simply wrap yourself with a clean, white sheet

You'll require at least one hour to perform the ritual. The best time of day to perform this ritual is dusk, as the day is turning to night.

STEPS FOR THE RITUAL

1. Construct the Altar

   • Turn on your meditative music.

   • Take several deep breaths. Clear your mind. Focus your awareness on your breath.

   • Light the smudge stick and wave it to clear the ritual space.

   • Prepare the altar in the middle of the space, with a white cloth covering it.

   • Place the bowl of clear water on the altar.

   • Light the incense and place it on the altar.

   • Place the flowers on the altar.

   • Dress the candle by using two to three drops of eucalyptus essential oil to draw a line from the bottom to the top on the white candle. Do this four times, at four equidistant spaces along the white candle. Place the candle on the altar and light it.

2. Prepare Yourself

   • Use Florida water to clear and cleanse your auric field by pouring a generous amount in your hands and sweeping your hands down the front and back of your body, swiftly and vigorously, without touching the body. Do the same over your head and under each of your feet.

   • Take a sacred bath. Add a generous sprinkling of salt and your rose petals to the bath. If you do not have a bathtub, use a large basin full of water to which you've added a tablespoon of salt and the rose petals. Take a shower first, then place the basin in the shower and wash with the sacred bath from the basin.

- Leave the bath or shower and pat yourself gently dry with the white towel.
- Don your white attire.
- In the ritual space, create a circle of salt on the floor surrounding the altar. Be sure you have all necessary ingredients inside the circle with you.
- Sit down at the altar.
- Pray or simply breathe. Meditate for twenty minutes on your intention to ascend, leave behind the old you, and be reborn as an ascended being.

3. Invoke the Elemental Spirits with an Incantation

- Earth: "Divine Spirit of earth, come!"
- Air: "Divine Spirit of air, come!"
- Fire: "Divine Spirit of fire, come!"
- Water: "Divine Spirit of water, come!"
- Ether: "I acknowledge the Divine in all, everywhere present as the active principle in me and birthing a new self here and now!"

Lay the besom in front of you on the floor. Close your eyes and take several deep breaths. Vividly imagine a new world in front of you, with your new spiritual identity. See and feel yourself as a new being. When you're ready, jump high across the broom with the intention of leaving one level of spiritual awareness and leaping into your new spiritual identity. This new spiritual you has an expanded and ascended consciousness and has left behind, on the other side of the veil, the old identity.

Pick up the candle. As you hold it, thank the spirit of fire by saying: "Blessed Divine spirit of fire, I thank thee. Walk with me always." Return the candle to the altar.

Next, pick up the smudge stick and smudge the new you. Thank the spirit of air by saying, "Blessed Divine spirit of air, I thank thee. Walk with me always." Return the smudge stick to the altar.

Then draw a flower from the vase. While holding it, say, "Blessed Divine spirit of earth, great mother, I thank thee. Walk with me always." Ask the flower for permission to use her petals for your transformation into one who serves the good of all. When you sense she has granted you permission, gently pluck the white petals one by one. As you pluck, place each one gently in the vessel of water. When you feel there are enough white petals floating in the water, thank the flower and lay her on the altar.

Lastly, pick up the vessel of water with both hands and gaze intently at the petals gently floating on its surface. Know that these petals represent your pure and heartfelt desire to empower yourself. State this incantation: "Divine spirit of fresh waters, carry my pure intentions to experience individuation and empowerment as an integrated being, and cause these intentions to be amplified and aligned with the universe and returned to me in the form of swift and elegant manifestation. Thank you, blessed spirit of fresh water." Return the vessel of water to the altar.

When the ritual is complete, ground yourself in the third dimension by eating bread and drinking water.

Go to sleep and awaken in the morning as a brand-new being, fully released of everything that has gone before that is no longer aligned with or complimentary to your greatest Divine expression.

DUMB SUPPER/FEAST OF THE DEAD RITUAL

A Dumb Supper is a meal eaten in complete silence—which is why it is called dumb—on All Hallows Eve, October 31. In this ritual, one's ancestors and other loved ones who have passed on are invited to participate, communicate, and offer messages in any form. You are opening the door to spirit realms and asking specific spirits to come through to share a meal with you.

Though it has been in use for ages, I've replaced the term "Dumb Supper" with Feast of the Dead.

REASONS FOR CONDUCTING RITUAL

- To establish a new connection with a recently crossed-over relative or someone who may have passed during the year since the last Feast of the Dead ritual.
- To deepen and clarify communication with ancestors and dead loved ones you're already connected to. This is a powerful ritual to expand communication and make it more visceral, meaningful, and clear.
- To determine which ancestor to call on, and for what purpose. My great grandmother birthed twelve children, of which eight made it to adulthood. If I were having a period of extreme grief, as I did when my mom passed over, I might call on great-grandma Pinky to ask how she managed to be the strong woman she was after losing so many children. When you have this kind of connection with each of your enlightened ancestors, you're better able to determine which one to call for the specific issue or magickal operation at hand.
- To make requests. Ask your ancestors and loved ones for what you require. Get supernatural help. It's available to you, and your ancestors have a vested interest in your complete well-being and ascension.
- To get rid of negative spirits. Negative spirits may be hounding you, in the form of persistent fears or spirits of jealousy or spirits of contention in a household. Enlightened ancestors are well-equipped and positioned to handle negative spirits.
- To honor, thank, and bless. Honor your ancestors. Thank your forebears for all they're doing in spirit realms for you and the world.

Bless them in their rising. Every candle we burn for our ancestors and every mention of their name keeps their light glowing brightly throughout all dimensions and powers up their spiritual essence.

You can make the ritual as elaborate or as simple as desired, according to your intuition and intention. It's ideal to conduct the ritual each year on All Hallows Eve. I've found that there are certain ancestors who will almost always show up, such as the ones closest to you, whether you specifically invite them or not. When you open the door to these close relatives, they don't need permission to come through—like my mom, who's always with me.

WHAT TO EXPECT

Because you are communing with the spirit world, you may experience strange occurrences and spiritual phenomena. There's no way of knowing exactly how the spirits will communicate with you—and others present—unless you speak with this ancestor frequently. The nature of this ritual is that you may be establishing communication channels with ancestors and loved ones you've never contacted since they've crossed over. This could cause interesting paranormal activity: technology in the home might flicker on and off, or completely stop working. You might experience a change of temperature in the room or smell familiar fragrances from departed family members.

SET YOUR INTENTION

Who are you contacting and why? What questions do you have? Are there prickly issues you're dealing with that you'd love clear guidance on? Is there an unresolved issue with your grandmother or another relative who has passed on? Are you at peace and just want to thank them for their obvious help in your life?

There are a plethora of honorable reasons why someone would want to speak with enlightened ancestors and loved ones on the other side of the veil. Include in your intention how you'd like the relationship to unfold going forward.

Write out your full intention in a grimoire or Book of Shadows. If you have neither, a notebook will do.

TIMING

This ritual is conducted on October 31 because All Hallows Eve is the night when the veil between this world and the world of the dead is thinnest, affording easier communication.

You can begin preparing for the Feast of the Dead well in advance, since you know when it will be each year. An annual observance will keep you in good stead with all helpful ancestors and will facilitate clearer communication throughout the year.

YOUR GUESTS

The ritual can be conducted alone or with company. If you choose to conduct the ritual with others, be careful that everyone you invite holds the same sacred intention: to honor their ancestors, create deeper and more meaningful communication, and generally gain help from beyond the veil for whatever manner of magickal working you might require.

Above all else, remember: This is not a dinner party. It is a magickal ritual that involves a feast.

If conducting the ritual with other witches, send invites to coven mates or members of your magickal community far in advance, or at least discuss it with them so that they, too, can prepare.

I've conducted my Feast of the Dead rituals alone, receiving powerful responses from my ancestors. You may be quite pleased and amazed at the outcome.

THE SPACE

Determine the location for your ritual. It could be a dining room or other space in your home, or it could be conducted in nature. If you have a magickal space where you or your coven gathers to do magick, this is perfect, as magick is already in the air and helpful spirits are already present.

The place where the feast will be held will need enough space for an ancestral altar large enough to contain the items and candles for each participant in the ritual. A large dining table works best if many participants are involved. You will set a place for each guest as well as one place setting to represent each person's ancestors.

If your feast will take place in a space not normally used for spiritual work, you will have to create sacred space for the ritual following the guidelines previously shared.

In this magickal ritual, you will be opening the portal to the other side and actively summoning spirits into the space. As with all rituals, creating sacred space—including cleansing and clearing, and calling in helper spirits such as angels, archangels, and spirit guides—is crucial for safety.

I recall attending the annual Samhain fire festival held by Wayne, a Druid and powerful shaman, in which he would open the portal at the beginning of the ritual so that those present had the opportunity to commune with ancestors and receive messages and guidance. He was a master at making sure all the spirits were back on the other side before he closed the portal.

Of course, you do not have to be an accomplished shaman to conduct this ritual. It is recommended that you be acutely aware of what you are embarking upon. Treat the entire process—the preparation, conducting the ritual, and completion—with the utmost respect, taking all appropriate steps to ensure excellent results.

PLAN THE MENU

Since the feast is held in the fall, foods of the season are best, including pumpkins, root vegetables, apples, and all manner of fall produce.

You will prepare an entire meal or feast, akin to Thanksgiving. If you're conducting the ritual alone, you'll prepare all the food yourself, or you can acquire the meal from a place you trust. Make sure to include on the menu drinks and foods your ancestors and loved ones enjoyed while they were in this life. This is critical.

I'm mostly plant-based in my eating, apart from fish. However, my mother and grandmother ate meat most of their lives. If you're a vegan and grandpa loved steak, have steak for grandpa and a vegan meal for yourself. Even though grandpa will not be eating the steak, as spirits don't consume human food, he will witness the representation of your love and the depth of your intention when he sees the steak. This is touching, just as it is if someone you love procured all your favorite things and invited you to dinner.

If others are joining you, have each person bring a dish. This goes a long way to make the ritual communal. As the food is being prepared, keep in mind that this is ritual food and should be accorded due respect.

CONSTRUCT THE ANCESTRAL ALTAR

On the day of the feast, each person participating will bring items representing their ancestors and loved ones to place on the ancestral altar, including pictures, if available. The ancestral altar can be set with sacred cloth in a color palette of fall colors, or deep hues of blacks and purples, or in white. Candles are placed on the altar to light just before the feast. You can dress the candles with favorite oils from your ancestors, if they have favorites that you're aware of, though this is not required. The colors of the candles are at your discretion, based upon intuition, your intention, and the ancestors involved. Keep in mind that all the lights will be turned off after the candles are lit and will remain off the entire time the ritual is being conducted.

Add to the ancestral altar items that come to you via intuition that may seem strange to your conscious awareness, like a stuffed toy bunny rabbit or the like. This may be a favorite childhood toy of a crossed-over ancestor. Pay particular attention to what arises from intuition about what to place on the altar, even when it makes no logical sense.

SET THE TABLE

The table setting is one of the most crucial factors of the ritual. It's important to have one place setting for each human being present, and one place setting for the ancestors and loved ones you will invite. For instance, you will have a place setting for yourself, and you will also set a place for your ancestors directly across from you—because the spirit realm is a mirror image of the physical realm. If your fork is on your right, you'll place the ancestral place's fork so that it is on the ancestor's left. When you look at the ancestral place setting, it should be an exact mirror image of your place setting.

A separate ancestral place setting is not required for each ancestor you seek to commune with. Consider the ancestral place setting as a doorway and invitation to spirit realms.

If you're seeking guidance from a particular ancestor, add that loved one's favorite food to the menu. When it's time to eat, you will put actual food on all the plates, yours as well as the ancestral plate. You will pour drink into your glass as well as in the ancestral glass.

A variation from this protocol is to prepare a place setting for each ancestor you are inviting if there are just one or two. When I've conducted a Feast of the Dead for my mom and grandma specifically, I had three place settings: one for me and one for each of them. Each cup held what they loved to drink while in this life: wine for mom and coffee for grandma. I had kombucha. This is a real meal with people you love.

If you're having a large gathering with others present, such as family members, it may not be possible to set a place setting for every human and every ancestor each person would like to commune with, which is where a "representational" ancestor place setting is useful.

As an aside, if you conduct a web search for "dumb supper" you'll see elaborate and beautiful, witchy tables that are magickly ornate. Some witches prepare the table and place settings for this ritual as if preparing for a wedding. Indeed, we are welcoming honored guests.

BREAK BREAD WITH THE ANCESTORS

When all has been prepared, it's time to break bread with the ancestors and spirits. Before sitting down to the feast, make sure everyone attending goes to the restroom. Treat the ritual as you would a magick circle: everyone stays put until the ritual is complete. When everyone is ready, bring the food to the table.

Everyone can then be seated at their appropriate place setting at the table, opposite of their own ancestral place setting, as the host lights the candles on the ancestral altar and then extinguishes all artificial light.

Turn off all electronics. If a television is in the room, throw a sheet over it. Television screens are portals, and All Hallows Eve is an active night for spirits, possibly the most active night of the entire year. Yet this ritual is specifically designed to connect only with ancestral spirits and loved ones you have specifically prepared and intended for.

The ancestral place setting acts as a portal directly in front of you for your ancestors to come through with powerful messages, answers, and solutions. They might even tell a joke or two.

Eat the meal in complete silence, keenly aware of everything happening in the room, especially sounds, smells, air movement, touches, impressions, and temperature changes, any of which might indicate supernatural activity.

COMPLETION OF THE RITUAL

When everyone has finished their meal and you sense that the ritual itself is complete, close the ritual. It should come to a natural conclusion. Everyone is likely to know intuitively when the ritual is over; some may have received several messages or insights from beyond.

You or someone you appoint can offer thanksgiving to the ancestors and bid them depart in peace, until meeting again. They know where their home is, so most will move along. If not, you can once again thank them and bid them farewell until all have returned to the other side. You will be able to sense this.

When everyone is certain all spirit activity in the room has come to a natural completion, clear the table in silence.

Do not throw away the food on the ancestral plates. The food is to be placed at the trunk of a tree, or in another place in nature, such as by a river or lake, if that's what your ancestors loved. I usually put ancestral food at the base of a tree with great thanks.

MY OWN FEAST OF THE DEAD RITUALS

I've conducted this ritual several times with profound results. On one occasion, my intention was to speak with my mom and grandma for guidance during an especially tough time I was experiencing. Because the mind latches on to ritual like few other events, I still remember so many details of this experience, including the exact place I was sitting in the room.

I happened to be living in a hotel that was paid for weekly, which gives you a glimpse into my financial situation at the time. There wasn't a kitchen to prepare food, so I acquired the meal from a store that sold high-quality prepared foods.

I bought items from Michael's craft store to dress the table—which, by the way, was not a dining room table but a low coffee table that sat before the room's couch.

Yes, this was a low-budget operation with no kitchen, which is exactly why I'm sharing my experience with you. It's not necessary to go over the top with cooking and other details, because the main point of the ritual is communication with loved ones. They would come even if we didn't have food. The food is a ritual offering representing our willingness and desire to have deeper, more meaningful and communicative relationships with them.

My low-budget operation also illustrates that anyone can do magick, at any time, with any materials on hand, if a powerful intention exists and the will is activated.

That night, I created a sacred space and carefully set three place settings: one for myself, one for mom, and one for grandma. As stated, I had wine for mom and coffee for grandma. I carefully dished out the food for the meal onto all three plates, just as I would have made their plates if they were in physical form.

I prayed, lit the candles, turned off the lights, and ate the meal in reverence and silence, waiting for them to answer, appear, or do anything.

They both showed up, and they had plenty to say. Yes, that's my mom and her mother. They didn't change as souls just because they had new addresses in spirit realms. They were full of wisdom and wit, as usual, and the whole affair felt familiar, like all the occasions when the three of us ate together on this side of the veil.

When the spirit activity was over, the ritual simply came to a natural completion. I've honored All Hallows Eve many times with ancestors, and each occasion was so profound I can scarcely put words to it.

It's my dream for you that you, too, have profound and meaningful occasions with your loved ones on the other side.

ANCESTORS IN THE MOTHERLAND

If we were in some parts of Africa, a Feast of the Dead ritual might not be necessary, as many of the ancestors are buried right on the family's land. The ancestors are with them every day, in every undertaking. When they leave the house, they nod at a great-grandmother, who may be buried in the front yard on the left. They're actively talking to her. They're teaching the children about Great Grandpa.

In cultures across African countries where there are no cemeteries and the presence of the ancestors is infused into daily life, having a Feast of the Dead might seem preposterous. Everyone there talks to their ancestors all the time.

However, for those of us in the west, who spend most of our time working and living in busy cities with our ancestors buried in distant places we might not have visited in years, conducting an annual Feast of the Dead can be a powerful way to strengthen and deepen the communication and the effects of the ancestors in this world.

Rituals are the witch's gateway to worlds beyond, including the realm of spirits. They can help give us access to ancestors, spirits of the land, and nature spirits. Our rituals are spirit-sustaining and revitalizing for the magick we wield.

The life of a witch is ritualistic in nature and form. This lifestyle is a spirit-charged way to honor seasons and cycles, elements, and ancestors—and all we care to emblazon upon our consciousness.

THE WITCH SEATED
AT THE TABLE

———•———•———•———

While leading a retreat recently in Dubai, we sat next to a large family from India. Several men wore turbans. At the same establishment were native Arab men with their traditional head coverings.

As a witch, I wondered what would happen if I wore a traditional witch's hat in these establishments. The reaction might not be as welcoming as would be the headdress of any other religious, spiritual, or cultural participant.

The witch hat is a symbol varying in meaning from person to person. For me, it symbolizes a conical channel of high frequencies, like an antenna. When we visit Salem, which we do often, we find stores stuffed with witch hats. During Haunted Happenings, an annual festival in the month of October in Salem, *everyone* wears witch hats. It is an acknowledgement that once witches were feared here, and that they are no more.

This is the vision I have for the world: a society in which the witch is not feared or maligned out of ignorance but welcomed in all her dark and light aspects as a powerful healer, teacher, and change-maker.

It is time for the witch to be positioned in her seat at the table of the world's religions and spiritual paths as a respected, honored member of humankind's varied approaches to the supernatural. Imagine the witch seated at the table respectably honored among all the spiritual paths of the world: Christianity, Islam, Buddhism, Hinduism, Zoroastrianism, Judaism, and all other faith walks.

The witch has arisen. Millions around the globe have heard and responded to her clarion call and activated their magick. Millions more are willing to do the same.

She's sent out the call to her own, and they have responded, across countries, cultures, religions, and languages, transcending the differences belonging to the mundane world.

It's not easy to be a witch. In some societies, witches are still feared. In others, we are turned to for help with all kinds of conditions. The witch as an archetype has touched us all for eons. It is deeply fulfilling to align with this primordial force when one hears the ancient call to magick and the moon and to nature and the elements. For the witches who walk this planet, an ancient magick stirs in our blood and bones that we are eager to answer and awaken.

The witch is an honored archetype, primordial force, teacher, guide, healer, and wayshower, as an emissary of the Goddess. May we all, in our own capacity, welcome and honor the witch with arms, hearts, and spirits flung wide open.

Blessed be,

Valerie Love

MEET THE SACRED STORYTELLERS

ANNETTE ASSMY, known as Chaskawisdom, is a storyteller, Cacao Guardian, mistress of ceremonies, and walks the path of a guardian of the earth (Pampamesayok). She is the founder of the Mystery School of the Soul. mysteryschoolofthesoul.com.

COLTON BERRY is a practicing Christian Folk Witch from Appalachia of East Tennessee. His own brand of magick is an eclectic path of Granny Appalachian Magic, Hoodoo, and Catholic Saint Work.

CHERKESHA SYLVINNIE CAESAR is a mother of three adult daughters. She was a member of Wicca World Coven and has traveled through many cities and states. She has lived a gypsy life, yet she experienced the beauty of nature.

EVA GALINDO is an energy medicine practitioner that has fought her calling for healing work since she was a child. A series of events led her to lean into her gifts to help others. iyaarialchemy.com.

ALTHEA GRACE is a writer, author, teacher, shaman, minister, prayer practitioner, intuitive, energy worker, witch, and lover of life, light, love, laughter, and liberty. berijoy.wordpress.com.

KMUR HARDEMAN is a storyteller, Feng Shui consultant, Reiki master, model, lover of the ocean, and all things magickal.

ENCHANTED HEALER is a Doctor of Oriental Medicine, Certified Western Herbalist, entrepreneur, and author. She is a high priestess of Hekate and lover of all things magickal. enlightenhealer.com.

ICY KENDRICK, aka Queen Moremi, is an acclaimed spiritual teacher, renowned psychic medium, and prolific international author. With her compassionate guidance, clients discover their innate gifts, overcome their shadows, and realize that death is simply a transition to the next phase of life. Her teachings inspire transformation and empower individuals to live their fullest potential. icykendrick.com.

ALY KRAVETZ, aka BronxWitch, is a witch, Tarot reader, Reiki master and owner of BronxWitch HeadQuarters–a spiritual shop and witchy work-share space in the Bronx, New York. bronxwitch.com.

DAWN M. KUBO uses her skills as a cosmic librarian, ascension activator, and her ability to access the universal libraries to assist you with finding and remembering the highest truth of who you are. cosmiclibrarian.info.

DONNA KUEBLER is a world traveler and multi-dimensional healer whose mission is to restore you back to wholeness and awaken your gifts. She's a channel, seer, shaman, Melchizedek priest, Akashic therapist, and witch who will help you feel more like you than ever before. thegoldenalchemist.com.

PAMELA D. NANCE has a master's in cultural anthropology, undergraduate degrees in archaeology and religion, and a 30 year career in social and biostatistical sciences. Pamela has researched the survival of consciousness after death for over 30 years and obtained certifications in healing touch, past life regression, shamanism, and spiritual dowsing. pamelanance.com

QUEEN VASHTI, a mother of three, a grandmother of four, and a mentor to many others. She entered this realm endowed with the Mother Energy. She hopes to be an inspiration to women and girls around the globe with a special interest in Africa, encouraging them to their greatness.

KJ WOLF is a flâneur, moving on this planet. She walks with eight medicine bags, a rich set of tools to teach, create, and heal.

MEET THE AUTHOR

Rev. Valerie Love, also known as KAISI, is an ordained minister of spiritual consciousness, practicing Christian Witch, and the author of over 20 books on practical spirituality, witchcraft, the occult, and the Magickal Arts & Sciences. As a teacher of occult studies, she founded the Covenant of Christian Witches Mystery School in the Solomonic Tradition to facilitate modern study, contemplation, and practice of ancient magick. KAISI teaches in the Mystery School at global retreats and events held in spiritually charged hotspots such as Sedona, New Orleans, Salem, Bali, Thailand, Dubai and Abu Dhabi, Peru and Mexico's ancient cities.

Since 2009 KAISI has taught Magick, Money, and Metaphysics to millions of viewers on YouTube. She has appeared on numerous television and radio shows, as well as podcasts, to teach a modern audience about the ancient mysteries, and that all have access to magick.

Growing up in the cult of Jehovah's Witnesses and breaking free after 26 years, KAISI has learned the liberating power of spirituality, versus seeking to comply with a religion. Thus, her walk and practice as a Christian Witch harmonizes the essence of Christ consciousness with magick and witchcraft for a soul satisfying life of service to humanity.

When she first exited the broom closet publicly as a Christian Witch in October of 2011 on her YouTube channel, she was shocked to discover the many thousands of others who felt the same way: witches who were unwilling to leave Christ and their Bibles behind. Armed with these realizations, she has been an outspoken advocate for witches and specifically for Christian Witches on YouTube, TikTok, Instagram, and Facebook, as well as on her podcast and in her series of books titled *The Christian Witchcraft Starter Kit*.

KAISI is a global traveler who explores, examines, and researches ancient cities and spirituality in destinations all over the globe, including China, Hong Kong, Thailand, France, Greece, Italy, Egypt, Kenya, Bali, Dubai, Abu Dhabi, India, Portugal and more.

She currently resides in a beautiful home in Mexico which serves as a home base for her travels as a global citizen.

Learn more at valerielove.com.